LEGENDARY HOMES OF THE MINNEAPOLIS LAKES

LEGENDARY HOMES OF THE MINNEAPOLIS LAKES

Photography by KAREN MELVIN

Text by BETTE HAMMEL

Minnesota Historical
Society Press

www.mhspress.org

The Minnesota Historical Society Press is a member of the Association of American University Presses.

Manufactured in China by Pettit Network Inc

Book design by Ellen Huber

10 9 8 7 6 5 4 3 2 1

∞ The paper used in this publication meets the minimum requirements of the American National Standard for Information Sciences—Permanence for Printed Library Materials, ANSI Z39.48-1984.

International Standard Book Number
ISBN: 978-0-87351-863-5

Library of Congress Cataloging-in-Publication Data

Melvin, Karen, 1954–
Legendary homes of the Minneapolis lakes / Karen Melvin, Bette Hammel.
pages cm
Includes bibliographical references and index.
ISBN 978-0-87351-863-5 (cloth : alk. paper)
1. Architecture, Domestic—Minnesota—Minneapolis. 2. Lakeside architecture—Minnesota—Minneapolis.
3. Minneapolis (Minn.)—Buildings, structures, etc. I. Hammel, Bette Jones, 1925– II. Title.
NA7238.M54M45 2012
728'.370977657—dc23
2012014730

For information on pages iv and v photos, see page 216.

For my mom, Alice.
—KM

To Dick: dear husband, father,
sailor, humanist, and pioneering
modernist architect.
—BH

*This book was funded, in part,
by generous donations from the
following individuals and companies:*

Victoria D. Abrahamson

Kathryn and Faruk Abuzzahab

Elna and Bill Campbell

Judy Dayton

John C. and Ann Dietrich

Dolly J. Fiterman

Hammel, Green and Abrahamson, Inc.

Hawley Family Foundation

John and Amy Higgins

Olivia K. and Jeffery D. Hornig

Gabriel Jabbour

Kathleen Jones

Terrence G. McGann

Scott and Sheila Mitchell

Sheila C. Morgan

Bob and Carolyn Nelson

Pamela and Jack Safar

John Skogmo

Streeter & Associates

Henry and Virginia Sweatt

TEA2 Architects

Emily Anne Tuttle

Pamela B. Vasquez

Philip H. Willkie

Renata Winsor

James Wittenberg

Kirtland C. Woodhouse

LEGENDARY HOMES OF THE MINNEAPOLIS LAKES

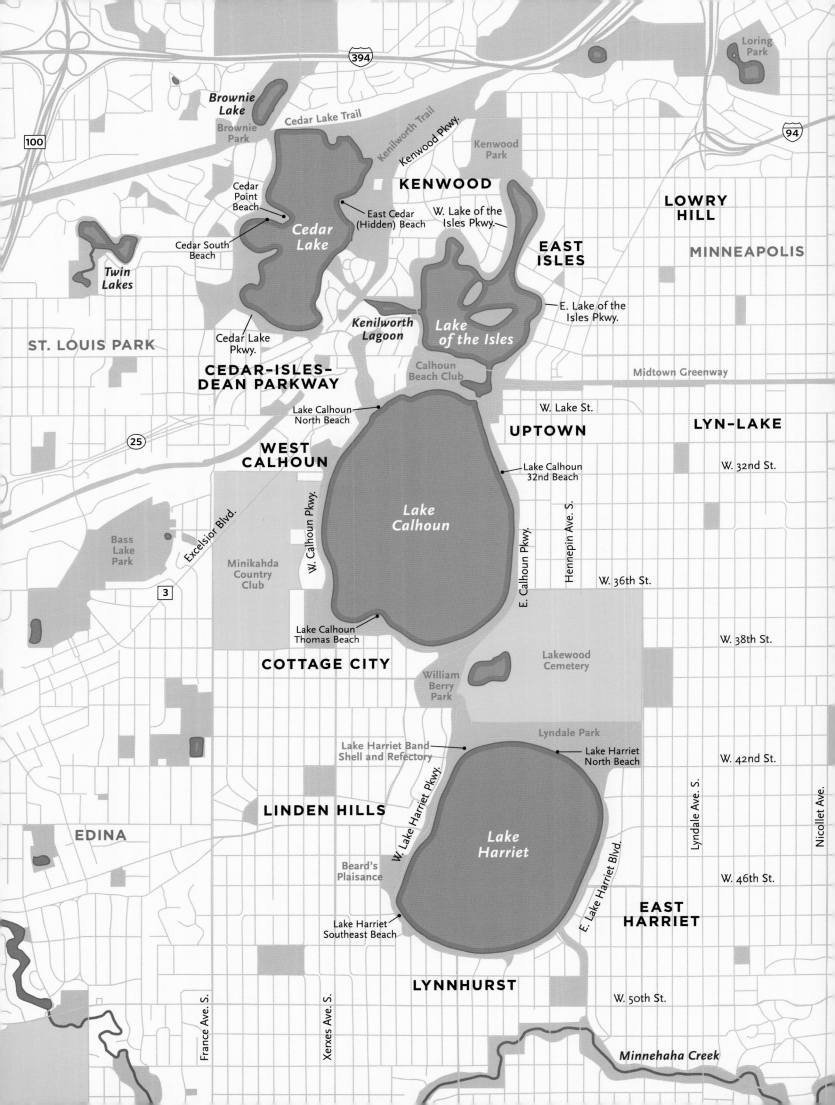

H ow about a walk around the lake? Sound familiar? Try this one: While you're walking or driving, or sitting in your favorite chair, how about taking an architectural tour around Lake of the Isles, Lake Calhoun, Lake Harriet, and Cedar Lake—the Minneapolis Chain of Lakes? This marvelous district, featuring more than thirteen miles of walking and biking paths, attracts over five million visits a year. And while people move around or across the lakes, they admire the distinguished homes, both old and new, on their shores. The pages of this book offer guided tours of twenty-six splendid homes and one remarkable neighborhood, all historically and architecturally significant. Thanks to their gracious homeowners, who enjoy living close to the Minneapolis lakes, we have seen these residences up close, both interiors and exteriors, and we are now able to share them with readers.

It's not surprising that the lakes are choice spots for building. For generations, Minnea-politans, St. Paulites, and suburbanites have loved this city's lakes. Not only because they're beautiful to look at, but because of the many opportunities they offer for outdoor recreation: swimming, sailing, canoeing, fishing. Biking, running, rollerblading, skating. Just plain sunbathing and picnicking. Or even—in the 1920s—watching horses race on snow and ice. Our landscaped public parkways have become a magnet for people of all ages, dog walkers and drivers. What other city in America is so blessed?

People have enjoyed these lakes for centuries. Mdewakanton Dakota families lived in nearby summer villages on the Mississippi and Minnesota rivers, which served as their highways; they hunted, fished, and gathered foods and medicines around the lakes in the appropriate seasons. In 1805 American soldiers negotiated with the Dakota for a military reservation; Fort Snelling was built in 1819 at the confluence of the Mississippi and Minnesota rivers, a place the Dakota called *Bdote* and considered sacred. Eight thousand acres of the former military reservation, including the Chain of Lakes, is now South Minneapolis. The Dakota, compelled to sign treaties ceding the land to whites in 1837, 1851, and 1858, were almost all forcibly removed from the state by the U.S. military after the Dakota War of 1862.

The two towns founded across from each other at the Falls of St. Anthony—St. Anthony, incorporated in 1855, and Minneapolis, in 1867—joined together in 1872 and began to boom. The immense waterpower of the falls drove sawmills, flour mills, woolen mills,

machine shops, and other industries. Between 1870 and 1880, the city's population grew by over 360 percent, to forty-seven thousand. With change so rapid, residents could see that they might lose access to the lakes if development were not planned. Over the objections of the city council, voters set up an independent Board of Park Commissioners in 1883. Charles Loring, a Minneapolis businessman, was its first president, and one of its first acts was to consult with Horace Cleveland, a highly regarded Chicago landscape architect. Cleveland convinced the fledging commission to plan a system of parks and parkways that would connect the Mississippi River and the city's lakes.

ABOVE: *As boats passed under a new bridge on July 5, 1911, Minneapolitians threw a grand civic party to celebrate the linking of Lake of the Isles and Cedar Lake. (Minneapolis Parks and Recreation Board)*

Other nineteenth-century visionaries assisted in the work, including William Watts Folwell, president of the University of Minnesota, Thomas Lowry, who owned the streetcar system, and William S. King, a farmer and U.S. congressman. Theodore Wirth joined them in 1905 as superintendant. They did not have a crystal ball, but they looked into the future and pictured a chain of sparkling lakes, of parkways owned by the people, of trees and greenery, of paths and trails for recreational use. Lands around many of the lakes were acquired in the 1880s, through many negotiations, heated arguments, confrontations, and compromises. Perhaps not surprisingly, landowners donated much of the land needed for the parkways. The landowners were also, in many cases, the developers, who realized that proper protection for the lakes would make them more desirable places near which to build.

For real estate developers, Lake Calhoun was a natural place to start plotting land development. It was the largest and deepest, with a good shoreline on its east side (although still marshy on the west side). Lake Harriet, though farther out from St. Anthony, would be a natural for development with its well-defined shoreline; Cedar, ignored in Cleveland's plan, was known for its rugged beauty. Lake of the Isles, however, was nothing but a mosquito-infested swamp. Once the lakes became more accessible, however, the city's new elite, the manufacturers and builders, could build beautiful homes on prime sites not far from their workplaces.

Well-qualified Minnesota architects were awarded the commissions to build such homes. In the late nineteenth century and early twentieth, they included Ernest Kennedy, who had studied abroad and also locally; Harry Wild Jones, a New Englander who became very popular here; and Purcell and Elmslie, with Chicago roots and inspiration from Frank Lloyd Wright. In the 1950s and 1960s, homeowners often chose locally based, well-esteemed Liebenberg & Kaplan, Edwin Lundie, and Close and Associates. In today's global markets, many Minnesota architects now work internationally as well as locally. Award-winning examples include Vincent James, Charles Stinson, David Salmela, and Tom Ellison. Their work, plus homes by several other noted architects, is seen in this book.

From the beginning, landscape architect Horace Cleveland provided the vision. "Look forward for a century," he said in 1883, "to the time when the city has a population of a million. They will have wealth enough to purchase all that money can buy, but all their wealth cannot purchase a lost opportunity, or restore natural features of grandeur and beauty." His vision was expanded in the years that followed, and Minneapolis became known as "The City of Lakes." Now the interconnected series of parks and parkways, known

RIGHT: *Races on snow and ice, popular in Minnesota since the 1850s, were a regular seasonal event on the ice of Lake of the Isles from 1886 to 1929. The lake was "conveniently close to the city," offered better shelter from the wind than Lake Calhoun, and provided good views from carriages on the boulevard. These trotters pulled sulkies on the lake in 1929. (Minnesota Historical Society)*

as the Grand Rounds Scenic Byway, is the country's longest continuous system of public urban parkways. Encircling the center of Minneapolis with a fifty-mile pathway, it makes the lakes and the lands around them accessible to the public today and for generations of Minnesotans to come.

All Minneapolitans who live anywhere near these glorious lakes are now enjoying the results of the visionary planning that began more than one hundred years ago. The homeowners described in this book say they love living on the shores of Lake of the Isles, Calhoun, Harriet, and Cedar, and they intend to preserve their homes for future generations. As you page through the book, note that each section begins with a brief history of the lake and concludes with notes about the landmarks. We list the residences in the order that you would find them as you move counterclockwise around each lake. Enjoy your tour!

Lake *of the* Isles

No one would ever guess that this enchanting lake was once a swampland breeding mosquitoes. It was Charles Loring, not Horace Cleveland, who foresaw Lake of the Isles' potential. In the late 1880s, he declared it was "one of the most beautiful spots in the city, and by dredging would be in reality a lake of isles." By 1893, the park board acquired the entire lake, and by 1889, it became the first major lake in Minneapolis to be re-engineered. A real estate boom soon followed, although more rounds of dredging continued until 1911.

As homeowners and their architects began building a distinguished neighborhood around the Isles, recreational usages increased. During the winters of 1897 through 1929, horse racing on the lake surged into popularity. Races were held every Saturday afternoon, run by horses drawing drivers in sulkies. Thousands of spectators cheered on the racers. Cross-country skiing and ice skating have also become favorite winter pastimes on the Isles, where the park board has maintained a large ice rink and warming house every year. In summer, the lake is a favorite for hiking, biking, jogging, and inline skating.

Of all the city lakes, Lake of the Isles has always been known as the most prestigious place for residences. Property values have consistently remained high, and the lake holds a large number of the city's most architecturally significant homes.

The Scriver McGann-Burke House, 1908

More than 105 years ago, Lake of the Isles was starting to attract homeowners, and city lots were turning over rapidly. The Scriver family, who ran a furniture business, and another family, the Tracys, together owned lots with 150 feet of frontage on the parkway, and in 1907 they decided the time had come to build. It made perfect sense for them to hire an architect to design two "sister" homes in one comprehensive scheme.

Their architect was Cecil Bayless Chapman, who had grown up in Minneapolis and became a draftsman for William Channing Whitney, known for his design of prestigious homes, and later Gottlieb Magney, also a residential expert. The houses share a common entry court. Because the Scriveners admired California houses, Chapman created a Spanish Mission Revival home, complete with red tile roof, rococo curves of the gables, brackets under the eaves, and minaret chimneys. For the somewhat smaller sister house, owned by the Tracys, he devised a slightly different image, exchanging the curving features for square and placing a pergola on the front exterior. Both homes were built with gray stucco façades. Because each owner wanted maximum views and sunshine, the architect sited the houses so that they diverge in front. The shared garage,

built in two distinctive halves for the two families, became an important feature of the landscape.

In the years that followed, many different owners occupied both houses, each enjoying close-up views of Lake of the Isles and proximity to downtown. The common entry court and the shared walkway, gardens, and garage have endured. But by the twenty-first century, the Tracy house had changed personality completely and became a glorified Italianate hybrid painted white, no longer a twin of its neighbor.

In 2002, however, local businessman Terry McGann bought the Scriver house, attracted by its history and graceful design. He and his partner, Jean , loved old homes and felt this stately structure, with its distinctive rounded curve projecting toward the lake, was the one for them. According to Terry, the house retained 90 percent of its original character, which they were determined to preserve. In one of

ABOVE AND OPPOSITE:

Terry McGann and Jean Burke, owners since 2002, hired Minneapolis architect Tim Quigley to direct the remodel of Cecil Bayless Chapman's original design. The side entry allows placement of the living room in front, affording the best lake views.

their best ideas, they changed the exterior color of the house from gray to a sunny yellow, thus reinforcing the Spanish Mission influence. They began remodeling the interior in 2003.

To direct the remodel, McGann hired Tim Quigley of Quigley Architects, Minneapolis, who has built a reputation for his fine renovations of older homes and other residential commissions. He also liked the home's side entry, because it meant the living room could spread across the entire space facing the lake—"a Frank Lloyd Wright idea," he said. The architect and crew began work on the entry hallway and living room. Outside the main room, on the rounded projection facing the lake, they built a curving outdoor terrace with wrought-iron railing, adding an attractive dimension to the landscape and making it accessible through the room's existing French doors.

The main feature of the living room is the original fireplace and its colorful Moravian tile surround. Rose and yellow tiles from the historic Moravian Pottery and Tile Works of Bucks County, Pennsylvania, set the color scheme of the room, featuring pale yellow walls, dark

OPPOSITE, TOP LEFT: *The heavy front door with arched window.* **OPPOSITE, TOP RIGHT:** *Colorful Moravian tile surrounds the fireplace.* **OPPOSITE, BOTTOM:** *Still another curve graces the top of the stairway.* **ABOVE:** *The Spanish Colonial living room retains the original fireplace.*

antique chests, comfy loveseat, and oriental area rug in similar colors. Jean Burke, who has an art history background, says the room could be described as Spanish Colonial.

The architects matched the Moravian tile in a new wider entry that opens to a hallway lined with historic photographs hung on a wall faux painted to resemble burgundy leather. An Arts and Crafts–style staircase lined with canine paintings leads to the second level, where the owners wanted a spacious master bedroom suite. Quigley gutted the space, providing a reading area by the fireplace and the curving windows as well as a walk-in closet and attractive new bathroom with freestanding tub. The owner added a handsome mahogany bed.

On the third floor, the former maid's quarters, the architect removed a wall to open up the space and improve access to the existing small balcony, where McGann enjoys stepping out to admire the lake vista.

The dining room is still the original, as are most of the wood floors, while the adjoining sunroom overlooking a landscaped backyard was remodeled as an office. "We needed to do a major job on the kitchen, however," said Quigley. To enlarge it, their work required removing the maid's stairway, then bumping out the exterior in order to give both owners an excellent view of the lake from their new breakfast table. This small addition provided an informal corner for dining and space for new appliances, cabinets, and modern systems. They also remodeled the butler's pantry, using reclaimed heart pine for the counters, and built in much more storage space. The charming light-filled kitchen now functions well for contemporary life.

OPPOSITE, TOP LEFT:
A freestanding tub in the
renovated bath. **OPPOSITE,**
TOP RIGHT: *McGann chose*
a mahogany bed for the
expanded bedroom suite.
OPPOSITE, BOTTOM: *The*
original dining room was
painted white, but its wood
floor was preserved. **ABOVE:**
The architect enlarged the
kitchen, adding a breakfast
area with lake views.

The original landscape plan for the house was well conceived, as the house sits above a retaining wall only forty feet back from the parkway but twenty feet above the street. A common brick walkway meets at the gardens where one can see the red-tiled roof of the shared garage with its unique oxeye windows, later duplicated in a matching new McGann garage.

This old house that has been completely renovated for life in the twenty-first century still radiates the warmth and cheer of those early times when Minneapolitans were just discovering the jewel that is Lake of the Isles. One can almost visualize the horses and carriages trotting by, the ladies in bustles and gentlemen in hats, or the young couples eagerly canoeing down the lakeshore. No wonder McGann and Burke, and others like them, are preserving these beautiful old homes. It's their gift for future generations.

The Clifford House 1931

In the early 1930s, America was still in the midst of the Depression, Prohibition was under way, the moving pictures industry had discovered sound, and Errol Flynn was often seen leaping across a castle floor, sword in hand. Perhaps inspired by the latter, George B. Clifford Jr. built an English Tudor Revival home on East Lake of the Isles Parkway. As son of one of the founders of the Cream of Wheat Company, he had the means to afford an impressively large home and hired Ernest Kennedy, the era's established architect of such homes, to design it.

The two-story house, completed in 1931, features two massive stone chimneys with tub tops reaching up to a tower that evokes eighteenth-century England. The Clifford family crest on the front door facing the lake also reinforces the period. The exterior façade is composed mainly of Minnesota's famous golden Kasota stone and is sheltered under a slate roof which has weathered well these past eighty years. Tudor motifs of stained glass are set into several of the clear leaded-glass windows throughout the first floor. Since the residence stretches over three quarters of the property, encompassing three and a half city lots, landscaping was kept to a minimum, except for the lawn around the house and mature trees. A low fieldstone wall originally surrounded the property.

OPPOSITE: *Architect Ernest Kennedy designed a true English Tudor Revival parlor, complete with vaulted ceiling and hand-hewn timber detailing.* **RIGHT:** *The home's exterior is clad in Kasota stone from Mankato, Minnesota.*

The present owners enjoy their views of East Lake of the Isles and the skating rink right across the parkway. To help preserve the land, they installed a wrought-iron fence around the estate.

Visitors step into a two-story English Tudor Revival parlor, complete with crown molding and plaster motif, hand-carved detailing, and period furnishings. Hovering over the adjoining staircase is a ribbed and vaulted oak ceiling. Down the hall from this historic space is a large, formal living room with a parge-work ceiling, a stone fireplace set against wood paneling, and a handsome Steinway piano built of mahogany.

When the owners bought the property from Thomas Moses in 1968, they had a large and growing family in need of more space. The house offered nine bedrooms upstairs and five fireplaces throughout, plus five rooms and maid's quarters on the first floor. The only remodeling they have done was at the initiative of the wife, who felt that the kitchen "was like a dark box with hallways" and needed to be completely modernized. In 2009, the couple commissioned Jim McNeal of De Novo Architects, Minneapolis, to redesign the area, which was originally the maid's bailiwick.

The architect took his cue from other formal rooms. "These English Tudor architects designed volumes such as an oval dining room, pentagonal sitting room, and rectangular entry hall," said McNeal. Therefore he and his crew removed the excess hallways and doors to create more space, reduced the size of the butler's pantry, and designed a rectangular kitchen featuring a ten-foot-long island topped with granite. Under the island they built in pull-out drawers, added new deep cupboards, and set the range into an alcove topped with a limestone carving. What had been a cleaning closet was opened up to become an inviting breakfast nook. Antique lighting

OPPOSITE, TOP LEFT:
The parlor's hand-carved stairway. **OPPOSITE, TOP RIGHT:** *The stone fireplace in the living room is flanked by the hand-carved Clifford family crest.* **OPPOSITE, BOTTOM LEFT:** *Seating in the parlor against the backdrop of the typical Tudor wood paneling.*

OPPOSITE, BOTTOM RIGHT: *Books reach to the ceiling of the oak-paneled library, and a secret stairway is concealed in the room.* **ABOVE:** *The spacious living room features a leaded-glass bay window with a Tudor stained-glass inset and plaster ceiling parge-work.*

fixtures were acquired from Architectural Antiques, while the white oak floor was re-stained in a dark coffee-colored shade to match the original colors used throughout the house.

Adjoining the kitchen was a small space for storing tools and the original maid's room, which was also remodeled to become a pleasant family/TV room. A fireplace trimmed with limestone to match the Tudor period adds character to this light-filled space. The architects also redesigned the octagonal stone entry leading into the kitchen from the driveway and garage.

The owner says his favorite room in the house is the formal dining room, which features a unique oval table made of inlaid mahogany, seating eight. He could not find a table of that shape, so he commissioned the Kittinger Furniture Company of Buffalo, New York, to build one. Leather chairs around the table suit the color palette of cream and Empire white with navy blue carpet. From this room, guests can enjoy vistas of Lake of the Isles. The most unusual feature of this part of the house is the pentagonal entry connecting the dining room to the foyer.

The library of the Clifford house retains the spirit of the 1930s, with oak paneling and shelves of books reaching to the ceiling, while comfortable leather chairs lend the genteel atmosphere of Old England. Both owners enjoy telling visitors about the room's secret stairway that leads up to a daughter's room and the hidden panels where they suspect liquor was stored during Prohibition.

That the English historical style of Tudor Revival became popular throughout America and has been carried on profusely around the Minneapolis lakes is not surprising, because people have grown to like the chimneys, gables, textured surfaces, intricate carvings, fireplaces, and towers—all elements that denote tradition, history, and security. These homeowners have now valued and preserved such features in their home for more than four and a half decades.

OPPOSITE, TOP LEFT:
An inviting breakfast nook occupies what was once a closet. **OPPOSITE, TOP RIGHT:** *The arch over the kitchen sink area helps to reinforce the home's period style.* **OPPOSITE, BOTTOM:** *De Novo Architects with Streeter and Associates completely remodeled and enlarged the dark kitchen, opening it up to light.* **ABOVE:** *The oval dining room also features a custom-made oval dining room table.* **RIGHT:** *A curving wall in the formal dining room provides an appropriate setting for the buffet.*

The Fiterman Skogmo-Morin House, 1950

Edwin Lundie, a native Iowan, became one of Minnesota's favorite architects after apprenticing with Cass Gilbert and Emmanuel Masqueray and then establishing his own firm, where he specialized in designing prestigious homes inspired by Normandy, Scandinavian, and Colonial American styles. Mix together French country houses, Scandinavian craftsmanship, and Colonial simplicity, and you get Lundie.

In 1950, A. M. Fiterman, a local Minneapolis liquor dealer, and his wife, Bertha Phillips Fiterman, selected Lundie to design a home on East Lake of the Isles. From the parkway, it appears to be straightforward Colonial Revival, but as its site is a corner lot, Lundie could extend the house toward the side street, massing its parts to appear more like a village joined together rather than just one house. Originally it was the site of the garden of a renowned mansion next door, now lost. After the death of Bertha Fiterman, several owners followed.

Today's owners, John Skogmo and Tom Morin, describe the style as a mixture of American Colonial with elements of Cape Cod together with a series of pods reminiscent of a French Breton village. They bought the house in 2002 and in 2003 began remodeling. They were delighted to own a Lundie house, sited so well and already noted for its fine craftsmanship, skillful organization, and beautiful detailing.

The house, as originally built, was connected to the garage via a breezeway that passed an open-air courtyard surrounded by gabled roofs. The smaller gable and massive chimney over the south ground-floor bedrooms wing disguises the large footprint of the house, which encompasses seven

OPPOSITE AND RIGHT:

Edwin Lundie, one of Minnesota's most esteemed architects, designed this landmark 1950s house. In a signature touch on the library's fireplace, he included a surround depicting a Chinese chess set against red and white tiles.

thousand square feet. The entire exterior is brick covered with a mottled whitewash; light blue shutters add accent. Wood-frame, double-hung windows, used throughout, provide the daylighting typical of a Lundie design. The Georgian Regency front entry features a transom-light door.

The plan of the house is extraordinary, revealing each appealing room, one after another. "You can look down from one end to the other end of the house. I call it 'enfilade,' a series of rooms, with doors all lined up in a row," says Skogmo. Ceiling heights vary from room to room. In the original portion facing the parkway, a forty-foot-long gallery hall lined with engaged columns leads from the entrance to the living room, noted for its bowed windows and newly decorated with cream-colored walls and handsome traditional furnishings. The room, warmed by a fireplace with carved wood surround, has an exceptional view of Lake of the Isles. A dentiled frieze by Aaron Carlson Millworks surrounds the ceiling and is repeated in other formal rooms.

For the wood-paneled library, Lundie added a playful feature, surrounding the fireplace with red and white tiles depicting a Chinese chess set. Tom Morin, an interior designer, notes that all wood in the house is still original, and in the library, "we had the pine washed and oiled and

stained to bring out the original beauty." Next to the library is a unique space called a stairhall, a Lundie trademark that is actually a small room at the foot of a staircase. A cabinet in the space serves as a bar.

In 2004, the owners completely rebuilt a garage and an outmoded kitchen at the back of the house. "We added fifteen hundred square feet of space from inside the house by opening up what had been the maid's kitchen," said Skogmo. Rehn Hassell of Yunker Associates Architecture, Minneapolis, handled the project, skillfully converting the old garage into a modern kitchen, twenty feet square, with French doors leading to the herb garden outside. The new space also allowed for an informal family room with modern furnishings but with deeply inset windows honoring Lundie. The porch breezeway was enhanced with pilasters, capitals, and French doors leading to the walled garden and the original part of the house. The turned-wood chandelier and a handsome coffered ceiling by Lundie still remain. The sawtooth trim over the door is repeated outside on top of columns along the walled garden. From the breezeway, the owners enjoy an outdoor sculpture court.

In 2004, they added a walled garden terrace, using the same whitewashed brick and creating a pleasant sunny retreat. The new garage reminiscent of Lundie's design was built in 2005.

Asked why they selected this house, Tom Morin replied, "I always loved the garden here, the way the architect organized the plan and the beautiful proportions." Summing up for both, John Skogmo emphasized, "I've always been fascinated by Lundie, so the idea of living in what I think is one of his masterpieces is a lot of fun." That's an excellent legacy, indeed, for the master architect.

OPPOSITE: *The wood-paneled library is one of Skogmo's favorite rooms.*
ABOVE LEFT: *Lundie's trademark stairhall room.*
ABOVE RIGHT: *Painted paneling and crown moldings frame the formal dining room.*
RIGHT: *A glass-enclosed porch breezeway forms a courtyard for sculpture.*

OPPOSITE, TOP LEFT: *A walled garden terrace with whitewashed brick creates a sunny retreat.* **OPPOSITE, TOP RIGHT:** *A modern family room, installed next to the kitchen, has bookcases and a window seat reflecting Lundie's style.* **OPPOSITE, BOTTOM LEFT:** *The 2005 conversion by YA Architects replaced an old garage and maid's quarters with a new kitchen.* **OPPOSITE, BOTTOM RIGHT:** *A narrow alley between house and garage.* **ABOVE:** *Architectural details in the casually furnished breezeway include a tray ceiling and wood chandelier by Lundie.* **RIGHT:** *YA Architects devised a clever way to maximize book storage space in the informal dining room.*

The Bull Higgins House 1928

During the early twentieth century, architect Ernest Kennedy became very popular among would-be homeowners living on shores of the Minneapolis Chain of Lakes. Classicism was his chief concern in design, and he carried out the style in a variety of nuances for his usually affluent clients.

One such client was Daniel F. Bull, president of the Cream of Wheat Company of Minneapolis and the son of one of its founders. In 1928 he commissioned Kennedy and hired a builder to create this Italianate structure with hand-carved stone features and a façade of buff-colored brick. Over the years, the three-story manor was occupied by many different owners who enjoyed entertaining in the generous spaces and took meticulous care of the property.

From the beginning, the parklike site near the corner of James Avenue South was very appealing, and the house offered superb views of the lake. The celebrated Bobby McFerrin, three-time Grammy winner and former creative chair of the St. Paul Chamber Orchestra, bought the house in 1994 and began using a room in the basement for his recording studio. Approximately three years later, however, when McFerrin returned to the East Coast, he sold the house to a new owner.

In 2007, John Higgins, a biotech executive, with his wife Amy and their two children moved back to Minnesota from California and began looking for a classic home in the Chain of Lakes neighborhood with walls large enough for their art collection. The Daniel Bull house offered just what they wanted:

OPPOSITE: *The formal entry demonstrates the Mediterranean influence in this classical residence, designed by architect Ernest Kennedy for Daniel Bull.* **RIGHT:** *The new owners, the Higgins family, began a renovation guided by the structure's architectural history.*

twenty rooms, obvious craftsmanship, and proximity to the lake. "We wanted to live in a vintage home with a proud architectural history, and we were especially inspired by classic Italianate architecture," says Higgins.

An outstanding hallmark of the architect's design is the grand foyer, an actual rotunda with gleaming marble floor and a huge fourteen-foot vertical window placed high above a winding stairway flooding the space with light. Three public rooms radiate from the rotunda, and a barrel-vaulted hallway leads to the living room.

Many parts of the house are original, including the windows; the woodwork, ironwork, and marble have been renovated. The paneling, shelving, and cabinets in the library, which were all refinished to show the original burled cherry wood, demonstrate the painstaking craftsmanship of the early carpenters. Floors are of oak. An unusual fireplace in this room is constructed of stone from the Mississippi River.

Just down the hall is the spacious living room, large enough for entertaining with live bands and dancing, with a refinished wood floor, modern furnishings, eggplant-colored draperies, and a custom sheep's-wool tufted rug. The room holds three impressive, timeless artworks, including an arresting 1928 painting by Rolph Scarlett over the fireplace. Adorning the eleven-foot ceiling are four original handcrafted stucco medallions and stucco lattice detailing. From this room, family and friends enjoy a clear view of Lake of the Isles and all the activity going on outside year round.

For the octagonal dining room, the Higginses commissioned a mahogany dining table, large enough to seat eighteen, and repainted the walls a deep bronze as an enhanced background for their paintings. They also hung a hand-blown Venetian glass chandelier.

A delightful sunroom of more intimate size—the loggia, as the owners call it—serves as another gathering space, with French doors opening to the gardens. Black wicker furniture upholstered in white shares the space with green plantings.

The extensive exterior renovations completed by the Higginses have direct Italian influence as a result of their trips to Northern Italy. The terrace flanking the front façade is grass, not hard pavement, and is lined with a row of low stone balustrades, a design feature inspired by the grand estates they saw around Lake Como, Italy (see frontispiece).

Although the kitchen had been updated by previous owners, the Higginses added more space, including a low breakfast table for their two young children, an adjoining family room with a television, and sliding door to the patio. In the rear of the house on the second floor, Higgins dropped the Italian motif in favor of twenty-first-century styling for his office and contemporary club lounge and media room, complete with colored lights and mirrored ball. The nine-thousand-square-foot home still has six bedrooms, eight bathrooms, and five wood-burning fireplaces.

Clearly the Higginses love living on Lake of the Isles' shores, where people are constantly jogging, biking, inline skating, or sauntering. "We used to live in New York," they say, "and it's like being in Central Park with a friendly neighborhood and a spectacular lake sunset view."

ABOVE: *In the sun-filled loggia: a unique table from Holly Hunt and a chandelier moved from the dining room.* **OPPOSITE, TOP LEFT:** *The library's unique stone fireplace.* **OPPOSITE, TOP RIGHT AND BOTTOM LEFT:** *The Higginses are avid collectors of timeless art, both modern and traditional.* **OPPOSITE, BOTTOM RIGHT:** *Walnut Corinthian columns frame the approach to the loggia from the living room.* **FOLLOWING PAGES:** *Tall windows in the living room flank the fireplace where a 1928 painting by Ralph Scarlett hangs. The interior design firm KBI Studios chose butternut sofas with colorful throw pillows.*

LEFT: *A custom-made mahogany dining table steals the limelight in the octagonal dining room.* **BELOW:** *A nineteenth-century Spanish Renaissance walnut table adds historical pedigree to the library.* **OPPOSITE, TOP LEFT:** *The classical revival front door leads to the lake.* **OPPOSITE, TOP RIGHT:** *John Higgins installed a media room and office for himself on the third floor.* **OPPOSITE, BOTTOM LEFT:** *Previous owners had updated the kitchen.* **OPPOSITE, BOTTOM RIGHT:** *The door opens to the lake.*

The Kerr Backus Barber House 1911

For the first time in the history of this hundred-year-old edifice, a family with children occupies the house. The original owner, Norman B. Kerr, a sales manager at Munsingwear, Inc., hired the architectural firm Kenyon and Maine in 1910. (After Maine left the practice in 1929, Kenyon did substantial work in Minnesota, chiefly as head architect for the Minneapolis, St. Paul, and Sault Ste. Marie Railroad for twenty years.) Lumber baron Edward W. Backus became the second owner of the house, remodeling and building a large addition in 1922. In the 1930s, Stanley and Peggy Hawks moved in and with great style entertained a multitude of friends devoted to the Metropolitan Opera. The fourth owner was a bachelor, Dr. V. Thomas Fallon, who bought many of the Hawks's antiques and enjoyed life in the prestigious house until he died in 2010. Through those years, Tim Barber worked for Dr. Fallon, managing the property and the doctor's other real estate holdings.

Barber inherited the doctor's estate. "He wanted me to have it because I understood and loved the house like he did," says Barber. The doctor also knew that Barber would keep it running and in good condition.

The Barbers were determined to preserve the house but make it more livable for their growing family. Through much painstaking work led by Barber, they have removed the dark heavy drapes, painted three main floor rooms cream, improved the kitchen, and refurbished rooms upstairs and in the basement.

OPPOSITE: *The formal entry, with marble checkerboard floor, demonstrates the Mediterrean influence.*
RIGHT: *The Mediterrean house at the James Avenue corner of Lake of the Isles Parkway.*

One part of the property they left completely original is the unique landscaping occupying three-quarters of an acre. Instead of the usual Minnesota backyard, the Kerr-Backus landscape carries you away to an enchanting Old World scene. "You feel," says Tim Barber, "like you're in Italy, Morocco, Sicily, or Tunisia." A Kasota stone walkway under a pergola laden with grapevines leads to the pool and pool house. A huge stone wall with stone columns, balustrades, and sculpted frogs surrounds the entire yard. Tall aqua-glazed urns topped with copper decorate the pool and walkway. The space is terraced toward the lake, and a colorful Italian-tiled fountain adds color to the large lawn. In summer, the Barber family enjoys the swimming pool lined with blue and white tiles and the European-style pool house that sits above it. The children love to climb up to the turret and deck on top. In back, four magnificent oak trees shade the area that leads to the carriage house–garage, a two-story building with chef's quarters above, matching the Mediterranean-styled house.

In renovating the interior, the Barbers retained the elegance of the sunken music room, where a grand piano sits on a raised platform at one end. Here, under a carved wood ceiling, was the Hawks's favorite place for entertaining. Tall casement windows light the handsome checkerboard yellow and white marble floor. Two steps up is the living room, with two camel-back Victorian

sofas facing another fireplace, antique furnishings, and French doors opening to a large terrace encircled by wrought-iron railings, where guests can enjoy excellent views of Lake of the Isles' sparkling waters.

Although the kitchen was still in workable shape, the Barbers made it more functional, repainted the walls and original breakfast room, and converted the back entry into a mud room. The adjoining dining room, which features the original large dining room table, was repainted in cream and opened up to the light.

The house's beautiful open entry hallway leads to the staircase and its wrought-iron railing with twisted spindles. Two huge windows light the area, which features an antique Guatemalan bench covered in red upholstery.

The three-story residence has four bedrooms and two baths on the second-floor and another bedroom with large storage space on the third. Dr. Fallon's office in the secondfloor library was kept intact, complete with his antique desk. A room in the basement is Tim Barber's favorite because it has such Old World character. Stone steps lead into a medieval-style room with a fireplace, stained-glass windows, and solid wood furnishings. At sixty-five hundred square feet, the villa itself is not especially large. "It's the garden that makes this house," says Barber.

While the present owners have subtly changed the house to suit their modern lifestyle, they have kept the spirit of European romanticism. You can still feel the glamorous days of the music recitals during the Hawks period and the scintillating drama of Dr. Fallon's dinner parties. Now it's a different story, a story of a young family enjoying every part of this estate: jumping in the pool, grilling outside the pool house, and feeling comfortable in a Mediterranean-style villa where the grand piano gets a workout from twin teenage boys.

PREVIOUS PAGES: *Stanley and Peggy Hawks often entertained stars from the Metropolitan Opera in this music room, added in Backus's 1922 remodel.* OPPOSITE: *An antique dining room side table and* Olivia and the Squire, *by W. P. Frith.* RIGHT: *Objects not to miss: A consol table from Guatemala and Italian eighteenth-century side chairs upholstered in yellow and cream silk.* BOTTOM, RIGHT: *A sixteenth-century Guatemalan bench and a large painting by an Italian portrait artist greets visitors.* BELOW: *An impressively tall window lights up the formal entry hallway and the stairway, which has a wrought-iron railing.*

ABOVE: *Two late-eighteenth-century American sofas in the living room, original furnishings, were re-covered in blue.* **LEFT:** *The grotto in the basement, with a hand-crafted stained-glass window, creates a cozy reading nook.* **OPPOSITE, TOP LEFT:** *An early nineteenth-century Dutch chest of drawers using inlaid marquetry technique.* **OPPOSITE, TOP RIGHT:** *An antique mirror adorns the fireplace mantel in the music room.* **OPPOSITE, BOTTOM LEFT:** *A grand piano, often in use, sits on the room's raised area.* **OPPOSITE, BOTTOM RIGHT:** *This rare 1770 English secretary fashioned from elm-wood was part of Dr. Fallon's unique antique collection.*

The Schutt Priest House 1897

A romantic Victorian named Mendon Schutt loved his bride-to-be so much that he built a house for her as a wedding present. The year was 1897. The site: a steep wooded hillside, high above East Lake of the Isles. The house? A snug slate blue and white Dutch Colonial, with the eaves of its gambrel shingled roof curving gently upward, like wings of a butterfly. Walter Keith, the original architect, published his plans in books and magazines, and he likely chose the design from an issue of his own *Keith's Magazine on Home Building*.

By 1926, needing more space, the family hired architect Ernest Kennedy to renovate and design an addition. They later built a detached two-story garage and acquired more land next door. Elizabeth Schutt, one of the two Schutt daughters, lived in the house throughout her life. She was active in the Friends of the Eloise Butler Wild Flower Garden, and she gardened extensively on the side yard. After her death in 1999, the property was sold to James Priest.

Local residents had always admired Elizabeth's gardens. When a sale of the house was announced in 2009, the current owners, who had admired the property for some time, quickly arranged the purchase, knowing the house needed extensive renovation.

ABOVE: *One of the oldest houses on East Lake of the Isles was renovated in the spirit of the original by architect Laurel Ulland.*
RIGHT: *The dining room enjoys light and lake views.*

To design the project, they chose architect Laurel Ulland, whose restoration work in Kenwood was highly praised. The new owners wished to completely renovate and modestly expand the house while retaining the original style and historic character. "We wanted to bring back the feel of the nineteenth century in a modern way, and from the beginning, we wanted to open it up as much as we could to the view," says one of the owners.

Ulland proposed a modest two-story addition, only ten feet in depth, to be built into the yard to the south of the building. In her plan, the house interior was gutted, reconfigured, and updated to include modern amenities and new mechanical, electrical, and plumbing systems. Workers installed new double-hung windows that matched those in the 1897 structure, rebuilt the sagging porch, added bays to the front of the house, and created an outdoor dining area on the front porch. By December 2011, following months of extensive reconstruction, the renovation was completed and the proud owners moved in.

The curving open-ended porch with its nostalgic white railing reveals a unique sweeping view of the entire length of Lake of the Isles. Trees remain on the steep hillside, where only the invasive varieties were removed and underbrush thinned out. Local landscape architects Sticks and Stones constructed a stairway connecting the home to the parkway below.

A bluestone path meanders through the half-acre side yard, which was totally reworked to provide additional planting beds and environmentally sensitive drainage control. A row of spruce trees, planted on one side for privacy, extends down the slightly sloping land. Because gardening is a major hobby for the owners, the landscapers saved the old perennial bed, then created

OPPOSITE, TOP LEFT:
*Up the original stairway
lies the 1926 addition, now
a modern family room.*
**OPPOSITE, TOP RIGHT AND
BOTTOM LEFT:** *The owners
enjoy a full-length view of
the shining lake from the
second-floor balcony and
from an expanded white-
trimmed porch.* **OPPOSITE,
BOTTOM RIGHT:** *With classic,
comfortable furnishings,
the living room overlooks
the porch and a new small
patio in back.* **ABOVE:**
*Visitors entering through the
custom authentic French
doors notice the impeccable
woodwork and detailing.*

mulched plots for other perennials, a new central garden, and a vegetable garden. Bluestone
pathways weave through the plantings, creating delightful walks. Two fountains with pools were
placed near the home's entry. "The whole reconstruction is like a mini-arboretum," said Michael
Saphir, owner of Sticks and Stones.

Visitors enter the house through a middle door on the newly screened porch and step into an
open entry. In the main floor reconstruction, the architect enlarged the opening between dining
and living rooms, expanding both natural light and views of the lake. Windows surround the
dining room and a new bay window opens off the living room. Comfortable new furnishings rest
before the fireplace with a grand piano in the background. The wood floor is partially original
and contains a combination of new and reused maple. The millwork, which is all new, mir-
rors that which was original to the house. For the dining room, the owners selected an antique
round maple table with an inlaid border from a local antique gallery.

Both of the owners enjoy cooking in the ample, sparkling-white kitchen. The broad rectangular
space stands out, not only for its design but for its spectacular views of the lake through a series
of windows above the sink; it also features a pale gray-green island topped with honed white
marble and soapstone perimeter. Interior designer Charles Uehrke of San Francisco, who also
designed the lighting throughout, describes the kitchen fixtures as industrial-style pendants
made of heavy glass similar to what is often seen in Belgium. He also illuminated a slim shelf

OPPOSITE, TOP LEFT: *Time out for relaxing high above the tree-lined bluff in the screened porch.* **OPPOSITE, TOP RIGHT:** *In the new master bedroom wing, the shower contains a surprise: mounted on the back wall is the original stained glass from the old front door.* **OPPOSITE, BOTTOM:** *Ulland designed this space with spectacular lake views as a true cook's kitchen.* **BELOW:** *The vintage wine cellar in the refinished basement.*

on the back wall to display the owners' pottery collection.

The original stairway was saved and given freshly painted white newel posts. It ascends to the 1926 addition, now a handsome family room furnished in russets and greens. On either side of the fireplace, the designers built in a narrow shelf for more of the owners' pottery.

A few steps up is a new amply sized master bedroom facing the lake vista, while a guest bedroom lies on the opposite side of a wide hallway leading to a new balcony overlooking the lake.

Downstairs, the decrepit basement was utterly changed. Highlighting the area is an all new vintage wine cellar entered through an arch hewed from the foundation's stone. The design also accommodates space for two offices and a family room with a Ping-Pong/pool table.

Outdoors, in the space between the house and garage, Ulland's crew built a new retaining wall, then a small cedar shake garden shed mimicking the style of the main house and original garage. The owners have already discovered some of Elizabeth Schutt's perennials, and they plan to rehabilitate the old garden in her memory.

Nostalgia simmers around this newly renovated home, now beautifully refreshed under its Dutch Colonial eaves, thanks to the owners who value the spirit of preservation and an architect who recognizes adaptive reuse as the theme of our times.

The Kenneth and Judy Dayton House 1997

A home reflects the owners' personality in many ways—taste, imagination, and the power to envision. Kenneth and Judy Dayton, a Minneapolis couple with a real love of art and architecture, hoped they would find a special architect, one with the soul of an artist, to create their new home. After completing an international architectural search, they selected Minneapolis architect Vincent James, appreciating his modern designs of residential architecture and realizing his passion for the project.

James, a native Minnesotan educated mainly in Wisconsin, began his career in New York and on the East Coast, then returned to Minnesota in 1984 to join HGA Architects and later partnered with architect Julie Snow in a joint practice. He had always loved the Modern movement as well as the great works of architectural history. In 1995, he founded VJAA, Minneapolis, with Jennifer Yoos and Nathan Knutson. The firm has enjoyed great success, winning design awards nationally and abroad; a significant commission in Minnesota was the Abbey Guesthouse at St. John's University in Collegeville. Early in 2012, the American Institute of Architects (AIA) awarded its 2012 Architectural Firm Award to VJAA, a national honor that is one of the most prestigious awards given by the AIA—a particularly significant accomplishment for a small midwestern firm.

The Daytons had already chosen a unique site, a slice of land culminating in a hillside overlooking the north arm of Lake of the Isles. James, in creating a minimalist L-shaped house that would fit the space, split the site asymmetrically, leveling the central ground area for a driveway, placing

OPPOSITE AND RIGHT: An Alexander Calder sculpture greets visitors at the front door of the Dayton house, designed by architect Vincent James. Guests enter the minimalist residence, composed mainly of glass and stone, through a teak entryway on an L-shaped courtyard.

the garage and service wing as a retaining wall, and making use of higher ground to find privacy from the street. Because his clients wished to protect their neighbors' views of the lake, the architect embedded the house into the site, creating "a part courtyard house and part belvedere." James worked in tandem with San Francisco–based landscape architect George Hargreaves to sculpt the site. On the lake side of the house, they planned a terraced lawn and curved plateau, which opens up a splendid long overview of Lake of

the Isles. Their strategy works like magic, because the plateau eliminates the sight and sound of the road and the bicycle and walking paths at the bottom of the hill.

As they began with James and his associates, the clients gave him a list of adjectives they hoped would be reflected in the architecture of the house: pure, warm, open, clear, simple, refined, elegant, clean, uncluttered, engaging, welcoming, happy, fun, light, airy, spacious not big, gentle, friendly, strong, radiant, sensitive, expressing delight, serene, quiet, unobtrusive, superb in every respect. Serene was the one adjective underlined.

From a distance, the house, completed in 1997, seems to be all glass, airy and light, graceful yet animated. As the architect notes, with a closer view, one can see that the two-story building is

actually made up of solids and voids as in a pavilion. A teak front entry welcomes visitors, and teak also covers the garage doors and terrace wall. The pale beige limestone from Indiana lines portions of the second-floor bedroom wing and the courtyard façade. Interior walls of the living/dining areas are almost entirely of specially designed low-iron glass, many with glazed pocket doors that slide out of sight. Here James collaborated with New York glass artist James Carpenter. In lieu of draperies, Carpenter also created louvers of movable wood and metal, part shoji and part Venetian blinds, that can slide open or closed.

Interspersed with the glass, white walls are hung with the couple's modern art collection, which adds colorful accents to the simplicity of the interior. The rectangular living/dining space serves well for many functions: family dining, dinner parties, larger gatherings, small meetings, and friendly conversations. A wall of books animates the space at the west end, acting as a closure for the "living room" centered around the fireplace. Furnishings are all midcentury modern and finished mainly in neutral shades.

In its conception and its execution, this tranquil house reflects the owners' overriding goal of serenity, matching the calm beauty of the lake it overlooks.

OPPOSITE, TOP: *An engaging sculpture by Claes Oldenburg adds whimsy to the scene.*
OPPOSITE, BOTTOM: *The terraced front lawn designed by Vincent James and San Francisco landscape architect George Hargreaves creates a place for two playful metal sculptures.* **ABOVE AND RIGHT:** *The Daytons asked for an expression of a happy, friendly atmosphere and especially a serene environment—an apt description, honored by James.*

The Mapes House 1914

Across the northern states of America, hot breakfasts on cold mornings are a favorite, and Cream of Wheat is a time-honored tradition on many tables. The steaming cereal was developed in 1893 at a mill in North Dakota co-owned by Emery Mapes, who later decided to build a lake home in Minneapolis. In 1914, he called on the popular Minneapolis architect Harry Wild Jones to design a proper residence for himself and his family in the already prestigious neighborhood of West Lake of the Isles.

The house was designed in the grand Renaissance Revival style (with Prairie School influence), complete with green tiled roof. Jones created it with his usual flair for glamour, function, and quality. With its Ionic columns announcing arrival, the eight-thousand-square-foot house originally contained fifteen rooms plus four fireplaces. Craftsmanship throughout was meticulous.

What followed, however, were years of bungled remodeling, an unfortunate addition, and conversion into a duplex, which destroyed the integrity of Jones's design. Even the glorious staircase was ripped out. By 1986, it had become an eyesore, and restoration expert Elizabeth Hyatt decided to rescue the home she had always admired. She bought the house and began a yearlong restoration, revealing a splendid interior and exterior for the next owner, Shirley Hutton.

LEFT AND OPPOSITE:

Harry Wild Jones pulled out all the stops designing this grand Renaissance Revival house for Emery Mapes. The current owners admired the way Elizabeth Hyatt, restoration expert, restored this house for Shirley Hutton.

After Hutton moved to California, the new owners, a Minneapolis physician and his wife, bought the house in 1997 as their family's residence. They loved the quality of the original construction, the solid Old World exterior, gleaming refurbished interior, and excellent views of the lake. Although they changed some of the wall colorings, they found the house suited their needs as a comfortable family home, with its beautifully proportioned rooms, restored curving staircase, and four spacious, well-lit bedrooms.

When first meeting Hyatt, the new owners learned how much the restoration work had involved. The exterior façade, including the brick and masonry, concrete-tile soffits, and balustraded balconies, was deteriorated from age and weathering. It took a skilled crew to repair the soffits, restore masonry throughout, add all new copper gutters, tear down a two-story 1940s addition, rebuild the porch, and repair the tiled roof. Hyatt commissioned ten thousand long Roman bricks to be custom made and cut to match the original. These were used for rebuilding the front porch and second-story terrace and for replacing damaged bricks. All original leaded- and stained-glass windows were repaired and reinstalled with new storm windows as well as new French doors replacing old metal doors. It was a massive job.

The interior was another major challenge. The restorer found that some of the woodwork had been destroyed or covered with gilt or green paint. Two fireplaces were missing their marble and carved wood façades. But it was the staircase that Hyatt yearned to return as one of the hallmarks of the residence. Fortunately, she discovered most of the walnut balusters in the attic, which meant that the woodcrafters could rebuild the solid walnut staircase that curves gracefully up to the second floor. A large geometric stained-glass window, found hidden on the third floor and now restored, highlights the landing.

Another outstanding feature is the foyer, one of the few areas of the house that had survived intact. Visitors are greeted in a high-ceilinged rectangular space lined with black walnut paneling. To the left, a comfortable living room with carved wood fireplace opens to a tile-floored solarium overlooking the lake. Curving leaded-glass windows, which the owners believe were inspired by the Prairie School architect George Maher, surround this special room, now a favorite reading room and nursery for grandchildren. A large formal dining room, refreshed with new paneling, fireplace mantel, and plastered off-white walls, features an inlaid quarter-sawn oak floor installed with herringbone pattern and border.

Today the restored home reflects its historic origins with modern conveniences added, such as an up-to-date, efficient, and roomy kitchen, a pleasant breakfast room with lake vistas, four and a half refurbished bathrooms, energy-efficient mechanical and electrical systems, and thermal pane glass covering the antique windows.

Asked about the perceived size of the original home, the owner says, "This is really a comfortable family house on a grand scale." His wife adds, "Now that our children are grown and bring their own children here, we feel the house envelopes us all and gives us space, either to be together or to find a little quiet retreat."

ABOVE: *Woodcrafters rebuilt the graceful walnut staircase.* **OPPOSITE:** *Curving stained-glass windows surround this sunny reading room, once Emery Mapes's office.*

ABOVE LEFT: *The formal dining room.* **ABOVE RIGHT:** *A carved wood fireplace centers the traditionally furnished living room, creating a cozy place for family gatherings.* **LEFT:** *Roman bricks that matched the originals were used to rebuild the front porch and second-story terrace. Note the four Ionic columns flanking the entry door.* **OPPOSITE:** *Harry Wild Jones took his cues from the Prairie School when he designed the art glass for the front door. Black walnut paneling lines the walls of the singular long entry hall.*

The Danaher Weesner Mitchell House 1911

The scattered residents of Lake of the Isles had something to celebrate one hundred years ago. Dredging had finally been completed in 1911, and the lake was successfully linked with Lake Calhoun. Thomas F. Danaher, president of a land firm company, thought 1912 was a year to build. He chose three lots at 2296 West Lake of the Isles Parkway, just where the parkway rounds a spoon-shaped tip of the lake. There his builder, Henry Parsons, devised a Tudor mansion of the period, with classic white stucco, half timbers, and a red-tiled roof—and one noticeable distinction. It was Swiss Tudor Revival, so called because the two matching gables are carved in sturdy oak and stand out like two gaily fashioned peaks against the sky.

Danaher lived there only until 1914. He then sold the property to Harvey R. Weesner, president of the Wabash Screen Door Company, Minneapolis. With his wife, two daughters, and son, Weesner moved into the fourteen-room home, where he resided until his death in 1942. His son, Donald Weesner, married and continued to live there with his wife. They had no children.

But Don Weesner had two other loves—pets and automobiles. The two-level stucco-clad carriage house, used mainly as a garage, also became home for three dogs, nine cats, and a squirrel. His classic auto collection grew, too, including models from 1925 to 1942 and, best of all, a 1929 Rolls Royce touring car ("Elizabeth") once owned by J. P. Morgan. The year after his death in 1998, the estate was sold to Scott and Sheila Mitchell.

The Mitchells quickly realized that renovation of the 7,750-square-foot structure was necessary. "The bones were good, but after a hundred years, the house needed updating," said Sheila Mitchell, who took charge of interior remodeling. There was no insulation, so they had the walls filled with twentieth-century insulation. New electrical, plumbing, heating, and lighting systems had to be installed.

The couple already liked the basic layout. Heavy wooden doors with stained-glass inserts lead into the oak-floored public entry. Straight ahead, a handsome cherry staircase ascends past a tall window, glowing with golden oak leaves worked in the glass.

ABOVE: *Twin hand-carved oak eaves mark this home as Swiss Tudor Revival.*
OPPOSITE: *A remarkable electrified newel post adorns the stairway.*

Like many of these traditional lakeside homes, the living room is on the left of the entry and the dining room is to the right. Surrounded by daylighting, the living room stands out for its cheery atmosphere and touches of color, such as gold and blue accents. Sheila divided this large space into two sections. The space facing the lake is comfortably furnished with a player piano on one wall and a classic 250-year-old grandfather's clock. On the opposite side of the room, facing the fireplace with its green marble surround, are two period sofas, end tables, a Tiffany-style lamp, and artwork. Walls are cream colored. Two large handmade carpets from Turkey rest on the original oak floors, enhancing each area of the room. An adjoining small sunroom (perhaps a former porch) accommodates a grand piano, plants, and other seating. The dining room is outfitted with an expansive inlaid oak-and-cherry table, with walnut base, seating ten.

Since the Mitchells have a combined family of eight plus two dogs, they use every bit of space, including the third-floor ballroom, which has been converted into an exercise room. There are four bedrooms upstairs (including a guest room with its original bookcase), seven fireplaces, and seven porches. The south porch now serves as an office.

The only rooms in the house that had to be completely changed, according to the owners, were the 1950s kitchen and master bath. The former was gutted and remodeled into an outstanding award-winning modern kitchen, designed by Lynn and Sandra Monson and fashioned mainly in cherry wood. Matching cherry cabinets incorporate stained-glass panels that echo the house's antique glass. The Mitchells worked to remain true to the original period, carefully reframing the windows and adding crown moldings around the ceiling and a floor of reclaimed oak.

Scott Mitchell, chief executive officer of the Mackay-Mitchell Envelope Company, often likes to read at home, where he can enjoy the lake views or the fireside, often concurrently. Sheila, a real estate agent and a mortgage broker, loves living in their old house. They are delighted with the journey they have taken to preserve the house for future generations.

BELOW: *A sparkling new, all cherry wood kitchen, designed by Lynn and Sandra Monson.* **OPPOSITE, TOP LEFT:** *A stained-glass window of golden oak leaves lights the staircase landing.* **OPPOSITE, TOP RIGHT:** *In the dining room. The Mitchells' black and white dog, Willy, is a half-brother to President Obama's Portuguese water dog, Bo.* **OPPOSITE, BOTTOM LEFT:** *On one side of the living room, the clock and piano.* **OPPOSITE, BOTTOM RIGHT:** *A vignette of green-tufted chairs.*

The Owre Willkie House 1911

In the grand sweep of American architecture at the turn of the twentieth century, two young draftsmen bent over their desks inspired by what they were learning from Chicago's innovative architect Louis Sullivan. Sullivan had sparked a drive to establish a new kind of American architecture that would celebrate our own land. "A building should unfold organically like a plant from a seed," he said. "It should suit its time and place like a river or a tree." By 1910, his draftsmen William Gray Purcell and George Grant Elmslie were ready to establish their own firm in Minneapolis. They had rejected the old European period revival styles of architecture in favor of the new Prairie School started by Frank Lloyd Wright and others. Residential architecture, they believed, should be based on nature, be simple and honest yet progressive, like the midwestern homes they were designing. In Minneapolis, they won many commissions, including one in 1911 from Dr. Oscar Owre. Thanks to those early visionary architects, the hillside site overlooking Lake of the Isles faces southwest, opening a wide view of the lake even though it is not directly on the parkway.

In 2007, Philip Heffelfinger Willkie seized the opportunity to buy his favorite architectural style in the Owre residence, then occupied by Nancy and Peter Albrecht. Since 1982, Willkie had studied the designs, toured a great many Prairie School houses, and particularly appreciated the linear forms and simple layouts of the style. "They must have been revolutionary," he notes, "to consider having an open floor plan and a living room that looks into the dining room with just a fireplace in between."

OPPOSITE AND RIGHT: *The rich wood trim of the hovering eaves and vertical front door identifies this Purcell and Elmslie house.*

FOLLOWING PAGES: *The original brick fireplace and hearth extend horizontally.*

Long before modernist architects stressed the importance of daylighting, Purcell and Elmslie were placing many windows in their residential designs, often grouping them together for maximum effect. This concept shines through in the Owre house. A series of six vertical wood-framed windows define the street-front façade of the house with a matching series on the second floor. Another set of casement windows brings southern light into the dining room.

Clad in pale stucco with dark wood trim for contrast, the house projects a feeling of American homeyness in the singular way that only these progressive architects captured. Perhaps that was the reason Oscar and Kathryn Owre chose Purcell and Elmslie to design their home. They loved it so much, they remained there most of their married lives. After his mother's death, their son Jacob remarked in 1955, "The house is still as honest and true as it was half a century ago."

A three-tiered brick walkway leads to a small entry where a cantilevered oak ledge protects visitors from the elements. Inside, a narrow wood stairway leads to the main floor, where the original brick fireplace stretches out horizontally, complete with hearth and a partial wall for art above. Mission-style wood furniture is casually placed around the cozy room with a comfortable sofa and cushions providing a more modern touch. Willkie's personal art collection adds color to the room. The structure's original wood floors, mainly oak, are accented with area rugs. Stretching across the front of the house, a pleasant window-filled porch now serves as an extension of the living room and creates an open vista of the lake.

OPPOSITE, TOP LEFT:
A built-in bookcase in the
living room. **OPPOSITE, TOP**
RIGHT: *Two white glazed*
replicas of Frank Lloyd Wright
sculptures from the Chicago
area grace the fireplace
mantel. **OPPOSITE, BOTTOM:**
Designer David Heide
renovated the old kitchen,
installing all maple-clad
cabinetry in the spirit of the
original. **ABOVE:** *The Prairie*
School dining room with
pendant lighting is furnished
with Willkie's mother's
dining room table and chairs.
Artworks prevail throughout
the house.

Tucked behind the fireplace, while still visible from the living room, is the simple dining room, typically furnished for the period with straight-back wooden chairs, oak dining table, and buffet. A bank of seven windows marches behind the dining set, affording diners a view of the picturesque side yard.

Nancy Albrecht, the previous owner, renovated the kitchen in 2006, commissioning MacDonald & Mack Architects, who had restored the Purcell-Cutts house on Lake Place owned by the Minneapolis Institute of Arts. David Heide, designer, retained the spirit of the period using the butler's pantry as a model and restoring kitchen cabinets to original specifications. The remodeling won a preservation award from the city's Heritage Preservation Commission in 2007. "No one has ever altered this house in a major way," says Willkie.

In their quest for providing shelter and a comfortable retreat, Purcell and Elmslie also designed a low-gabled roof that hugs the Newton Avenue house and added a similar soffit over the porch. In 2011, the one-hundred-year-old roof finally succumbed to damage from windstorms over the years and had to be replaced. A new cedar-shingled roof gives the house a golden hue, as though to say, "Look, we're here for another one hundred years." Exterior landscaping also needed work, according to the present owner, so he and a friend planted new flower gardens and extended an architect-designed fence that surrounds the backyard.

As the descendant of Minneapolis's well-known Heffelfinger family and grandson of Wendell Willkie, Philip takes an active part in local civic and community affairs. With a lifelong interest in architecture, he now feels he has learned to understand the philosophy of the Prairie School architects led by Sullivan and Wright who rejected European architecture and gave America its own style. He is proud that Purcell and Elmslie started their architectural practice right here in Minneapolis, designed so many outstanding projects, and helped to change the direction of residential design.

The Ford House 1929

The spirit of Pennsylvania Dutch lives on in the Ford Colonial Revival house on West Lake of the Isles Parkway. The white shingled house, with its forest-green shutters so reminiscent of the early American period in history, held great appeal for the new owners, who bought the house in 2000. Another major incentive was its prominent site, set back from the parkway by a broad rolling lawn, giving the house a splendid vista of the lake. As owners, they soon found they owed it all to Mr. Ford.

Allyn K. Ford, a Minneapolis businessman whose company was best known for Mrs. Stuart's Bluing, loved everything Americana. The descendant of a pioneer Rhode Island family, he collected American letters and manuscripts. He became so successful that in 1929, he selected his brother-in-law, architect Clarence W. Brazier of Philadelphia, to build him a fine Colonial house. Brazier took great care to design a large home suitable for a man of Ford's status and in keeping with the characteristic features of Pennsylvania homes of the Revolutionary period. The Minnesota chapter of the American Institute of Architects presented him an award for one of the best residences erected in the state in 1929–30.

Subsequent owners made improvements, beginning with the Cyril Pesek family, who lived there for thirty-one years. They refinished the oak floors and repainted the exterior with a fresh coating of white. Pesek was a well-known architect, engineer, and manager at 3M. By 1996, the Kozloffs owned the property and promptly set to work remodeling the back of the house, including the old kitchen. Jan Kozloff Heasley hired builders who helped her enlarge and convert the space into an efficient working kitchen. She also brought the original Cotswald cabinets up from the basement, painting them Wedgewood green to match the home's Colonial atmosphere. The space was enlarged to include a wooden breakfast table and a built-in desk. An interior hallway was broadened and lined with glass to reveal views of the backyard.

When the current owners took over, the house still projected an appealing traditional feel of Americana. A spacious foyer greets visitors over gleaming wood floors, and just opposite, a handsome wood staircase with Colonial spindles winds its

ABOVE: *Architect Clarence W. Brazier of Philadelphia used old Virginia hand-split whitewashed shingles and green shutters for the façade of this Colonial Revival house, built as the home of Allyn K. Ford.* **OPPOSITE:** *Colorful Russian art accents this historic home.*

way upstairs to four bedrooms and three baths. Neatly tucked under the staircase is a powder room and small storage space. The family of five especially appreciates the front and back staircases, which make it so convenient to move around the house. Another major feature near the foyer is a Dutch door leading to the backyard.

The Ford house was built with a high level of craftsmanship, and the interior woodwork is notable throughout for its carved designs, unique in each room. Ceilings in the living and dining rooms feature crown molding, while the library ceiling complements the swags of Wedgewood plaster on the woodwork. All floors were constructed of three-quarters-sawn oak.

There are six fireplaces (all framed in Delft tiles) and three chimneys in the house, but the family uses only one fireplace nowadays. Next to the spacious, traditionally furnished living room is a semicircular library, complete with fireplace and comfy seating and wholly paneled in Wedgewood

OPPOSITE, TOP: *A wooden staircase with Colonial spindles winds past a Palladian window.* **OPPOSITE, BOTTOM LEFT:** *The main dining room, with its own fireplace, offers glorious views of the lake.* **OPPOSITE, BOTTOM RIGHT:** *An etched colonial lantern hangs from the plaster medallion over the stairway.* **ABOVE LEFT:** *The current owners, a family of five, enjoy meals on the sunny enclosed porch.* **ABOVE RIGHT:** *Arches, crown moldings, and simple decorative windows predominate.*

green. One can visualize scholarly Mr. Ford working on his papers in this charming room featuring a curving wooden door and two curving windows looking into the backyard.

The dining room, placed to the right of the front entry and in the front of the house, boasts a broad view of the sparkling lake beyond. The room has been repainted in a rose color, another 1930s prevailing touch. Two arched French doors flank the fireplace, one fronting a china cabinet and the other opening to a screened porch.

Especially popular rooms for the family are the two porches that anchor each end of this house, which is noted for its symmetry. The south porch (with sleeping porch above) is the outdoor screened-in type, while the north two-story porch is lined with storm windows and overlooks the backyard.

The exterior of the house is clad with old Virginia hand-split shingles, all whitewashed to contrast with the green shutters. As is typical in Colonial homes, all the chimneys are also whitewashed with matching chimney flues. Windows cross the upper and lower façade in regular formation, all using little panes of glass set in small frames, while vertical styles prevail alongside the porches. The main entrance, reached via a sidewalk with a wrought-iron railing, is paneled, painted dark forest green, and topped with a semicircular arch.

In this residence, Brazier achieved a highly symmetrical picturesque neo-Colonial home that has retained its early American influence down through the years.

ABOVE: *Five fireplaces were built into the house, including this one in the traditionally furnished living room facing the lake.* LEFT: *Wedgewood plaster swags adorn the library's woodwork.* OPPOSITE: *The library, the most charming room in the house, features a curving wall of windows and doors.*

The Martin House 1915

When the sophisticated Parisian couple first arrived in Minneapolis in 2008, they were immediately impressed with the natural beauty of the city's lakes and parks. Lake of the Isles especially appealed to them for its walkability, its undulating shoreline, and its stately old homes. Like so many house hunters of the past, they confined their search to Lake of the Isles and soon found a home that matched their expectations.

The house, an elegant Italianate villa reminiscent of the Villa del Lago in Northern Italy, was built in 1915 for Gerald R. Martin, secretary of the Brooks Elevator Company. The architect, James A. Burner, was reportedly from a Chicago firm. Because of the narrow shape of the parcel, the main entry does not face the lake. Clad in sunny yellow stucco and surrounded by a wrought-iron fence and gate, the villa casts a prominent façade along Penn Avenue. Visitors enter the inner courtyard, then walk up a stone stairway to a landing and up again to the main entry. The owners greet visitors from a foyer noteworthy for its classical arches and columns and the original black and white terrazzo floor. Adjoining the entry is a formal staircase, where a huge gold-framed mirror dominates the landing. All the public spaces, restrained in size, are on the main floor stretching from one end to the other. Facing the lake is the homeowners' favorite space, a delightful sunroom with arched windows above a small Italian courtyard surrounded by greenery and flowering plants.

Fortunately for the new owners, the previous owners, William Kirchner and Mike Bratholdt, had restored the entire structure. "In 1994, when we moved in, it was still 80 percent of the original, but nobody had done much to the house except decorating a little," said Kirchner, former executive vice president of product development for Department 56. They began by repairing the leaking red-tiled roof, then replacing the pink stucco with yellow, a major improvement. "I could not live in a pink house," said Kirchner. They worked for two and a half years to restore the interior to its original Old World Italian character.

OPPOSITE: The original black and white terrazzo floor of this Italianate villa, flanked by classical columns, stretches across the main level. RIGHT: With its entrance on the street side of the narrow lot, the home offers scenic views of Lake of the Isles.

The remodelers also built a new back wing for the house, sorely needed to expand the eight-by-ten-foot kitchen. The original open porch was screened in and became a full-size breakfast room, and the butler's pantry was stained in nutmeg to match the existing wood. Beyond that, they added a small mud room and backyard entry. As a major part of the renovation, they even excavated under the house to create additional space for a two-car garage.

The present owners found they needed only to change some of the wall colors. The living room became a very pale pink and the dining area azure blue. Their art collection hangs throughout the house, adding a lovely European touch. Next to the original fireplace are two matching loveseats upholstered in a tiny blue and white pattern.

On the ground floor is another favorite place for entertaining. At one time, the wood-paneled room had a mahogany dance floor and bar. The new owners kept the bar but use the dance floor space for furnishings. Guests can easily step out through new French doors into the front garden from this pleasant room.

OPPOSITE, TOP LEFT: *Tall Italianate windows highlight this crimson-covered Empire sofa in the sunroom.* OPPOSITE, TOP RIGHT: *French artworks, brought by the new owners, add color to the room.* OPPOSITE, BOTTOM LEFT: *The hallway along the butler's pantry.* OPPOSITE, BOTTOM RIGHT: *The heavy gilded mirror at the foot of the landing has remained in place since the house was built.* BELOW LEFT: *The present owners changed wall colors, using pale pink in the living room and a blue chair for accent.* BELOW RIGHT: *The architect cleverly balanced the villa's façade at the corner facing the parkway.*

As Europeans transported to a strange environment, the French couple appreciates the neighborhood and its proximity to Lake of the Isles. They enjoy walking around the lake and watching people jog, bike, and canoe in the summer and cross-country ski or skate in the winter. "People here are very friendly," they say. Perhaps silent thanks should go to the vision of Minneapolis's nineteenth-century park board, which planned the beauty that has brought people from around the world to live along the shores of the city's shining blue waters.

OPPOSITE: *Corinthian columns frame the elegant staircase in the entry foyer.*

ABOVE: *Light filters through a Palladian window in the sun-filled living room.*

RIGHT: *The charming living room offers perfect proportions and smaller-scaled furnishings.*

The Amsden Sandbo House 1922

One of the early homes designed by Liebenberg & Kaplan was an English cottage–style house with wraparound shingled thatched roof hovering over a white stucco façade. It was a popular design in 1922, adding a quaint look along West Lake of the Isles Parkway. The first owners, Mervyn H. Amsden and his family, must have enjoyed living in their picturesque cottage, actually a version of Tudor Revival inspired by the vernacular cottages of sixteenth- and seventeenth-century England.

Jack Liebenberg was already a busy architect by then. Having graduated in the first class of the University of Minnesota's fledgling School of Architecture in 1916, he earned a master's degree at Harvard, then returned to the University of Minnesota and soon founded his own firm. Liebenberg, Kaplan and Martin became one of the most successful architectural practices in Minneapolis, designing several Jewish temples, including Temple Israel; many movie theaters (some Art Deco in style), including the Suburban World, Varsity, and Uptown; and a number of outstanding homes.

In 1972 the third owner of this Lake of the Isles cottage sold it to local businessman John Sandbo, his wife, Mary, and their young family, who were attracted by the design and especially its proximity to the city's chain of lakes. The Sandbos undertook some remodeling, updating a 1930s kitchen and attending to the roof. After Mary Sandbo passed away, John Sandbo married Jean Thomson, a technical writer and daughter of a well-known realtor.

OPPOSITE: *Jack Liebenberg designed this picturesque English cottage–style house in 1922.* **RIGHT:** *The crest of Mervyn H. Amsden, the original owner.*

Thomson, an architecture buff herself, loved the house immediately and was soon welcoming visitors through the multi-columned entry. Here the architect brought the house's singular feature, the bent shingled roof, downward as though to hug the entry. Since the roof is so unusual, Sandbo has made painstaking efforts to ensure its future. "It was beginning to wear out in the seventies, so by the eighties I knew we had to start over," said John.

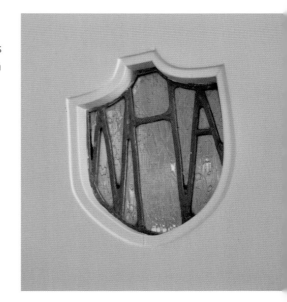

Bent shingles are made by steaming the cedar shingles so they will bend over the edge of a roof. Then they must be laid in uneven rows to simulate thatch. Sandbo learned that although many local factories produced this kind of shingle material in the 1920s, none of them survived. Only three companies in the United States still made or repaired this kind of shingle. "I knew it would take a specialist for the job, and it turned into an eight-week effort," he added. The cost was forty thousand dollars in 1982. Since then, the owners, using a local firm, have had to replace a little over a third of their uniquely shingled roof. But it's worth it to them, they say, because it helps to preserve the Old World character of their home.

The couple also appreciates the way the architect planned the interior of this three-level home. "The main floor is like one continuous room, except for a raised level for the sunroom," says Thomson, who likes the way this plan allows freedom of movement. The living room flows off to the left of the entry, with dining room on the right. But the sunroom, which has the best view of the lake, is Thomson's favorite. She calls it her reading room. Traditional furnishings, splashed with reds and blues, are grouped around the fireplace, with a grand piano opposite. The space radiates a charm that seems built into this house.

ABOVE LEFT: *The lake from the front entry.* ABOVE RIGHT: *Seating in the foyer.* LEFT: *The living room, traditionally furnished, exudes a charm that pervades this house.* OPPOSITE: *A polished stairway leads to the second and third stories.*

OPPOSITE: *A blue and green chinoiserie patterned wallpaper highlights the dining room.* ABOVE LEFT: *The cheery sunroom, a favorite place for reading.* ABOVE RIGHT: *The house is connected to the garage via skyway, which doubles as Thompson's office.*

Daylight pours into the dining room, which is flanked on both sides by banks of vertical casement windows affording wide vistas of the lake's west bay. This delightful blue and white room is wallpapered in a blue and green chinoiserie pattern and has a scrolled white ceiling. Upstairs are three bedrooms and baths, a study, and a third floor that contains a former maid's quarters, now a separate bedroom and bath.

In 1996, the owners gutted the old kitchen and replaced it with a cherry-paneled modern kitchen, complete with new appliances, granite countertops, heated floors, and a breakfast room overlooking a colorful flower garden. In a china closet, they kept the original emblem of Amsden, the first owner, as a symbol of the house's history. Besides the breakfast room, the couple also included a new back-door entry, closets, and powder room in the addition.

Another unique feature is what Sandbo calls "the first skyway in Minneapolis," built in a 1935 addition that connects the house to a bedroom and bath over the garage.

Adding to the romantic aura of this house is a beautiful flower garden on the front lawn, featuring many perennials, black-eyed susans, and hydrangeas and, in spring, many tulips and daffodils. The architect beautifully sited the house on a hillside overlooking the Peavey Fountain, a longtime favorite in Kenwood that dates back to the horse-and-buggy days, and a splendid view of Lake of the Isles.

"We love that the house is known as the mushroom house, reflecting its distinctive roof style," says Thomson. Indeed, it is only through the diligence of committed homeowners, now and in the future, that this unique feature of this remarkable house will be preserved.

The Twenty-First Century House 2010

In 2010 Lake of the Isles' first twenty-first-century house was built high above the historic parkway. For seventeen years this savvy young couple had lived happily in an old house on Lake of the Isles. But when a neighboring early-twentieth-century home burned down and the crumbling house next door to it became available, they saw an opportunity to create a dramatic new home and bought the combined property. It was a big decision, but as two people with imagination and creative instincts, they already knew a great deal about contemporary architecture: edgy, dynamic, and open to nature. This was the kind of home they wanted to build.

They decided to use local talent for every aspect of their new house, starting with the architect. After seeing examples of Tim Alt's contemporary award-winning designs (including a home on White Bear Lake, among other projects), they chose his firm, Altus Architecture+Design, Minneapolis, and were convinced that Alt could help them realize their vision. Shane Coen of Coen+Partners was also retained as the landscape architect.

The design team's initial challenge was to organize the house within a narrow buildable area and integrate it within the neighborhood. After studying the character and scale of the neighborhood through photography and context models, the team decided to design the house as a "family of structures" that would reflect the rhythm and fabric of the neighborhood's existing homes. The architect described this approach as "progressive contextualism, creating a hierarchy of forms and expressions that respect the variety of homes nearby." This concept involved both pitched roofs and flat, a green roof, and garden areas acknowledging the parkway context. Inspiration for the architecture also came from the Glasgow School of Art by Charles Rennie Mackintosh in Scotland.

OPPOSITE: *In this striking black and white setting, the Formula 1 race car that won the 1964 Grand Prix in Monte Carlo steals the show.* **RIGHT:** *Composed of a "family of structures," this new complex, designed by Tim Alt, stands out as the first truly contemporary house on Lake of the Isles Parkway.*

In shaping the site, the designers created a series of terraced gardens and large open space for family activities on the lake side of the property. The original perimeter stucco wall on the street was replaced with a black granite wall as a base to the gardens and plinth for the house to rest upon. A stairway of black granite weaves through the terraced gardens leading up the entry. "The reshaped site re-establishes an urban edge, a landscape buffer to the parkway below," said Alt. After the parkway walls and granite steps were finished, the owners called in Damon Faber Landscape Architects to help soften the edge by planting shrubs, trees, and grass.

Working closely with his clients, Alt divided the house into three parts: the public spaces on the south, family spaces in the center, and the garage and guest spaces to the north. A glass link connects the public and family areas. Together, they agreed to use only three materials for the exterior: stone, metal, and glass. Dazzling ivory Dolomite stone from Wisconsin clads the house in contrast to the black granite used for the landscape, walls, and steps. The metal roof is built of bronze anodized aluminum panels. For this contemporary setting, glass predominates, affording the owners with great views of the lake, yet the landscape provides a sense of privacy from the street.

Following completion of the exterior in 2009, the owners brought in an interior design team from Perkins & Will, Minneapolis, led by interior designer Michelle Hammer. According to Hammer, their basic concept was to bring the outside in, highlight the drama of the public spaces, and create family-oriented spaces for the domestic wing. "We also wanted to incorporate functional art as part of the living space, as well as contemporary artwork," added the owner. On the entry granite floor, for example, a P&W staff artist composed a sandblasted etching of leaves and flowers executed in a subtle style.

In the tall living room, where glass walls reach up two stories, daylight pours in, illuminating the contrast with the black floor and ceiling. The result: high drama set against wide-open vistas of the lake. Furnished primarily in black and white with crimson accents, the room is used mainly as entertainment space by the owners. Two white leather sofas tufted with tiny red stitches and a red rope-based glass-topped coffee table overlook the lake. A dark-stained, hand-scraped walnut floor adds even more contrast to the setting. Sliding doors lead to an outdoor patio furnished with white dining table and matching chairs. A cube-like space holding the master bedroom hovers over a portion of the high-ceilinged living room, creating room below for a small library. The most noted attraction in the room is not a painting but an actual Formula 1 race car, the winner of the 1964 Grand Prix in Monte Carlo, hung like a sculpture over the gold Venetian plaster wall.

Across the center link and two steps up is the formal dining room with a color palette of black, silver, white, and blue. The dining table rests on a patterned cobalt blue and white carpet, and contemporary art hangs on the silver Venetian plaster wall. Highlighting the space are two glistening chandeliers designed by a New York jeweler.

ABOVE: *A Minneapolis artist, Josie Lewis, created a unique countertop for the kitchen island by pasting together layers of collage.* **OPPOSITE, TOP LEFT:** *A sandblasted etching of leaves and flowers on the granite floor of the entry foyer.* **OPPOSITE, TOP RIGHT:** *A small library off the living room is defined by a cube-like structure supporting the master bedroom, overhead.* **OPPOSITE, BOTTOM LEFT:** *Library detail.* **OPPOSITE, BOTTOM RIGHT:** *On an elevated section of the living room, a black table with chairs overlooks the patio.* **FOLLOWING PAGES:** *Sunlight in this singular living room.*

Another sliding door opens to the family's private spaces: the kitchen, breakfast area, and family room. The large square white kitchen features a unique artisan-made countertop. Created by Josie Lewis, a Northeast Minneapolis artist, the counter is covered with many tiny cutouts of magazine pages layered in resin and laid out in a circular pattern like a kaleidoscope. For the breakfast area, a semicircular space wrapped in glass, while the kitchen opens to a comfortable family room.

A nearby spiral wood stairway, artfully adorned with black beading and unique lighting, leads to a second floor, which includes two bedrooms, work area, and wide-open studio specifically planned for the owner's artistic projects. Square bedroom windows, designed by the architect, are cantilevered out from the wall so that family members can climb out and sit "within" the window and enjoy panoramic views.

On the third level on the public side of the house is the other owner's studio, featuring space for film editing, business projects, and a collection of his mother's antiques. Hammer, the interior designer, says, "It's like a Parisian attic." The space seems to open magically to a deck and tiered seating of bronze anodized aluminum. Family and friends love to sit out here and enjoy watching activity around the lake. Another studio door leads out to a flat green roof, planted with sedum, with additional space for outdoor entertaining.

The owners occupied their new home in October 2010, and they now express satisfaction with their "out-there" kind of new architecture, a daring statement of contemporary design set into a traditional neighborhood. The owners comment, "We believe if those who built homes around the lakes were building today, this is the kind of architecture they would choose to build. They were bold and beautiful in their architectural choices of the past, and we have no doubt they would have been so today as well."

ABOVE: *A spiral stairway next to a west window highlights black hanging pendant lighting and black beaded screening.*

OPPOSITE, TOP LEFT: *Michelle Hammer and the owner designed this airy powder room with pink butterflies dancing against a white background.*

OPPOSITE, TOP RIGHT: *Twin chandeliers strung together with glass, beads, and jewelry hang over the dining room table.*

OPPOSITE, BOTTOM LEFT: *Black, silver, white, and blue form the dining area's color scheme.* **OPPOSITE, BOTTOM RIGHT:** *In the powder room off the dining area, a mosaic mirrored wall was designed by local artist Sharra Frank.*

OPPOSITE: A fine spot in the office for enjoying the view. **ABOVE:** The office space, inspired by a Parisian attic, opens to a metal deck and sloped roof with stadium seating. **RIGHT:** The film editing space for the owner's business projects.

The Hall Weiner-Wittenberg House, 1979

The late architect James Stageberg always loved the touch and scent of wood. In the many modern homes he designed, he created wonderful wood dining tables, beds, benches, bookcases, cabinets, shelves, and stairways. And he didn't stop there. On the rooftops of many homes, he also built wooden platforms, safely enclosed with railings, to provide views of the natural surroundings. A warmhearted, likeable man, Professor Stageberg was a favorite among his university architecture students, who learned how to become modernist architects and how modernism with its focus on simplicity and timelessness would reshape the world.

Among his various clients, Rosalie (Rody) Heffelfinger Hall stood out. A philanthropist and Episcopal minister, she commissioned Stageberg to design for her a special house near a corner where Sheridan Avenue meets West Lake of the Isles Parkway. Hall wanted it to be distinctive yet understated, with sufficient wall space for books and art and a deck for entertaining. The result, completed in 1979, was a three-story, all-redwood, modernistic classic, angled just right for clear views of the lake. She got not just one deck but three terraced decks, culminating with a crow's nest on top.

In 2006 the house was sold to James Wittenberg, an attorney, and his wife, J. Pam Weiner, a psychologist. Both admired the way Stageberg built attributes of modernism into the house

OPPOSITE: *The living room of this redwood modernistic classic is encased in oak paneling and punctuated with vertical windows.*
RIGHT: *Designed by James Stageberg, the home is sited just right for a clear view of Lake of the Isles.*

and the way the structure nestles quietly into the neighborhood. "James preferred to use clean, graceful lines that didn't intrude," says Stageberg's widow, Susan Allen Toth. The Wittenbergs made few changes except for the kitchen, master bath, and outdoor areas.

A highlight of the interior is the living room, punctuated with tall vertical windows and paneled in white oak that reaches up twenty feet to the ceiling (also of white oak). Even the chimney is clad in wood, soaring up from the fireplace as though going out of sight. Works by 1960s artists like James Rosenquist, Frank Stella, and Jim Dine decorate the walls. A Japanese kimono hangs high on the east wall and a rug from Istanbul on the west wall. Tibetan temple banners hang in the top of the living room's distinctive curve. Wood shelving holds books and various objects brought back from travels abroad.

Dining space is located in an open great room, also dominated by white oak floor trim and ceiling, where Hall had inserted stained glass into a semicircular row of smaller windows on the south wall. The adjoining original small kitchen needed an update. The Wittenbergs selected Tom Meyer, principal of Meyer, Scherer & Rockcastle, Ltd., Minneapolis, to redesign the space. He retained its galley shape but extended its length by removing a front entry closet. Using wenge, a dark wood from West Africa, for cabinets and reeded glass for cabinet doors, Meyer chose art glass for the kitchen counter and a wider reed glass backsplash to reflect the spirit of Hall's original leaded-glass windows. A similar seven-foot-wide glass panel slides over the

counter to hide the kitchen when the owners entertain at the dining table. The main floor also accommodates Pam's office, the laundry, and the entry to the garage.

The second level holds three bedrooms, two baths, and two walk-in closets. The all-white master bedroom with built-in cabinetry overlooks the lake and a "Juliet" window that peers down into the living room. All second-floor rooms have white oak trim.

Since this house was designed to be close to nature, the architect provided three decks, which are great spaces for relaxation and entertaining. The roof deck is large enough for thirty people to move around, enjoying food and wine while admiring the view. To take even better advantage of the lake vista, the Wittenbergs lowered the railing of the main floor deck. In the front yard, a new water feature, created for this space by Courtney Epperly of Urban Escapes, features two tall basalt column fountains over a large basin of Lake Superior stones. Boulders, sedges, and perennials finish the street-side landscape.

The Wittenbergs have created the outdoor spaces on this rather narrow lot to complement the inspired architecture of this home. Pam, who is president of the Friends of the Wild Flower Garden (the Eloise Butler Wildflower Garden in Theodore Wirth Park), focused on native plants as much as possible, while observing practical ecological solutions. Native plant guru Judy Remington, of Temenos Gardens, designed all three garden areas. The back of the lot has a sunny side with a kitchen and herb garden, a clematis-covered fence line, and a fragrant lavender bed. On the shady evergreen side behind the kitchen deck, a large rain garden was installed with downspouts from the flat roofs channeled to tubing under the bluestone walkway.

These gardens act as an extension of the home and its natural feeling, its abundance of wood, inside and out, and its rich exposure to light and views of Lake of the Isles.

ABOVE LEFT: *The first modern artwork that greets visitors is Ada Four Times by Alex Katz.* **ABOVE RIGHT:** *A work by James Rosenquist stands out above a slim console table in the hallway.* **LEFT:** *A bookcase offers ample spaces for artwork and books.* **OPPOSITE:** *A semicircular row of art glass clerestory windows surrounds a built-in bench in the open great room.*

The Smith Liepke House 1911

The horizontally oriented homes of Frank Lloyd Wright's Prairie School, reflecting the undulating hills of the Midwest, caught on rapidly in the early twentieth century, and Wright became the nation's most famous architect during those years. Other architects began to echo the designs. In 1911, a Minneapolis father-and-son architectural team, Dorr & Dorr, designed a large, prestigious house for a client on an inviting site of West Lake of the Isles Parkway. The original owner was John W. Smith, businessman and district manager for Air Reduction Sales; his family was followed by three other owners of the house.

The Smith house was distinctive at that time for its broad horizontal Prairie School form, clad in stucco with a sheltering hipped roof of Mediterranean flat red tiles. It had the usual front porch, ample living and dining rooms, three bedrooms upstairs, and plenty of daylight throughout. The interior had an Arts and Crafts mode with dark wood trim and wood floors.

What attracted an artist and his wife to buy it ninety years later? Skip and Michelle Liepke could see it had been well built and had a good plan flowing through the rooms. They began to visualize the possibilities for their family. The previous owner had installed air conditioning, new plumbing, and a furnace. Skip Liepke, a prolific figure painter of note whose work is shown in many galleries in New York, Los Angeles, London, Telluride, and Hong Kong, had a finely tuned color sense. The Liepkes knew they would immediately change the existing color scheme of pink walls and mint green carpeting.

The couple sought out an architect who specialized in older homes for the renovations they envisioned. Joseph G. Metzler of SALA Architects Ltd., who had rehabilitated many such historic residences, began work on the house in 1991. Liepke chose the color palette for the entire house, using mostly autumnal shades of pumpkin, forest green, gold, and soft beige. Having visited many Frank Lloyd Wright homes throughout the country, he was inspired by the famed architect's drawings to design all the art glass in his historic home. The dining room and foyer now feature Liepke's original designs for Prairie School overhanging lamps, with smaller versions in the living room. Original 1911 lighting fixtures remain outside and on the front porch.

ABOVE: *This one-hundred-year-old house, Prairie School in form, was designed by Dorr & Dorr Architects.* **OPPOSITE:** *The sunny breakfast area, with glass doors opening to a patio.*

Metzler and his associate, Steve Buetow, did a complete remodel of the kitchen because the original was very small and had not been updated since the 1920s. Metzler described the remodel as Arts and Crafts with Prairie School and Craftsman influences and the kind of detailing the owner wanted. The result is an expansive all-wood kitchen featuring gleaming reddish mahogany cabinets and an island topped with green slate countertops and complementary wall tiles. The artist-owner, who chose the colors, also designed the transom lights in the kitchen windows and custom light fixtures, while the architects designed the ceiling decoration and improved connections to other rooms. They linked the kitchen to the formal dining room, for example, by dropping the ceiling in the pantry. They also created a lower level casual breakfast

area and connected this space to a hallway and mud room leading to the newly attached garage. Liepke painted the lower level a pale orange and covered the metal knobs in the kitchen with a bronze patina. The kitchen is now forty feet long, including both levels, and spatially relates to the traditions of the Prairie School architects.

The 1929 sunroom located in the back of the house, surrounded by a curving wall of windows, was remodeled by the Liepkes as their family TV room, complete with built-in benches along the window wall. The artist maintains his own studio on the lower level and displays some of his favorite artists' works throughout the house.

Another renovation by Metzler involved the front porch, which needed new insulated windows and a custom-made front door with art glass. For the wood stairs leading to the second level, the architects raised the stairway windows high enough to create a light-flooded landing at the top.

Landscaping was the final renovation. In 2001, the Liepkes bought the property next door, took down the house, and designed an Asian-inspired garden, working with New York landscape designer Dennis Piermont. Minnesota winters have not been kind to some of the Japanese plantings, according to Skip Liepke, but the bonsai trees and spruces still decorate the gently sloping hillside and add an all-green enhancement to the Lake of the Isles Parkway. Since the front steps leading to the home's main entry were crumbling and in disrepair, SALA architects created new concrete steps, accented by planters designed in Wright's style, leading to the main entry.

"Houses are living things," says Liepke. "They all go through changes, like this house; it's still evolving, like a work in progress."

The Purdy Winston House 1911

The indefatigable Harry Wild Jones was riding a tide of architectural successes in 1911 when he designed a stately Arts and Crafts–style mansion for Judge Milton G. Purdy. From its site high above the western embankments of Lake of the Isles, the tall, cream, stuccoed house with its green gabled roof now proudly proclaims its one-hundredth anniversary. Built as a spacious abode for the family of the distinguished Judge Purdy, who served in several state and national posts, as well as an international one in China, the house later sheltered Frederick and Elizabeth Winston and their three sons for fifty-two years. Today, a family of four thoroughly enjoys the three-story historic home, handsomely restored inside and out.

In 2000 the current owners began working with Minneapolis architect Andrew Porth (now of Red Lodge, Montana), who had built a reputation for quality residential design. They soon realized the old house needed a complete restoration. In fact, portions of the house had settled so much that they had to be jacked up into place. To replicate the stone base, Porth found limestone from abandoned bridge pilings. Much of the original stucco was still in good shape, but it required some patching. Both limestone chimneys remained stable, while the tile roof had to be replaced with new green-glazed clay tiles duplicating the original.

Along with the restoration, the owners required a major addition in the back of the house, which included a new kitchen and family room, an exercise and mud room downstairs, and a new two-car garage. A new carriage house with a guest room apartment and additional garage space was built along the driveway in the northwest corner of the property.

OPPOSITE: *Architect Harry Wild Jones designed all the art glass in the leaded-glass windows of the entry and throughout this stately building.* **RIGHT:** *Many chandeliers grace this restored mansion, sited high above Lake of the Isles.* **FOLLOWING PAGES:** *The home's outstanding outside entertaining space.*

Most important, this is a home where art plays a lead role in the design. Jones, an architect of many talents, designed all the art glass in the tall leaded-glass windows of the entry, dining room, living room, sunroom, stairway, and kitchen. The mainly geometric designs are extraordinary: delicate, whimsical, and beautifully suited to the modern interior design of the restoration. During the restoration process, all the art glass was painstakingly removed, cleaned, and carefully set aside until reinstallation. Remaining windows were replaced with new insulated glass. While the owners are avid collectors of contemporary art, they have chosen works that accent rather than detract from the historic character of their home.

In the living room, for example, two oversize pieces hang on one wall, while another work hangs above the fireplace and a contemporary sculpture stands near the window. A charming window seat upholstered in blue and black tones fills a large bay window overlooking the terrace gardens. The floors and most of the wood trim in the house are of dark-stained oak and complement the blue motif.

The original enclosed porch became known as the sunroom. This was Elizabeth Winston's special place, where she spent much of her time reading, enjoying the lake view, or visiting with

OPPOSITE: *Interior designer Martha Dayton selected a smoke-colored leather sofa by Christian Liagre, flanked by two white mohair barrel chairs by John Hutton for Holly Hunt.* **ABOVE:** *A stained-glass ceiling lights up the second-floor landing, which serves as a gallery space for the owners' contemporary art collection.*

grandchildren. A row of the original windows still encircles this sunny room, bringing in many vistas of the island across the lake and the energetic walkers, bikers, and joggers who pass by. According to Frederick Winston, her son, she also kept a carefully penciled list of all the dates when the lake froze each winter and thawed each spring, pinned up in her closet. Fortunately, the current owners saved her historic list, and they continue the tradition of noting the ice-in and ice-out dates on Lake of the Isles.

The kitchen originally consisted of four separate rooms, each serving a different function. It was completely remodeled with SieMatic cabinetry as one big open Euro kitchen with sinks at the windows, a large island of stainless steel, maple, and marble, new appliances, and a breakfast area. The new family room, a prominent part of the addition, lies partially open to the kitchen and is comfortably furnished with tables by Edward Farell and Lewis Mittiman, chosen by designer Martha Dayton.

A large dining room adjacent to the kitchen holds a round table that seats ten. All chandeliers throughout the house were replaced with newer fixtures suitable for the period. Considering its era, the amount of daylight that was originally accessible in this house is remarkable.

Stepping out the back door in summer, guests encounter an outstanding outdoor room, complete with dining table and chairs resting on a concrete platform built over the garage. At ground level, landscapers created an attractive patio, where comfortable new wicker lounges flank a coffee

OPPOSITE, TOP LEFT: *In the sunroom overlooking the lake, Elizabeth Winston, whose family lived here for forty years, took note of the lake's changing seasons.*

OPPOSITE, TOP RIGHT: *Three Mr. Benny club chairs in gray from Holly Hunt surround a coffee table in the living room.* **OPPOSITE, BOTTOM LEFT:** *An occasional chair by Rose Tarlow was re-covered to complete this vignette by the walnut fireplace.* **OPPOSITE, BOTTOM RIGHT:** *An Arco lamp bends over the dining table in the new family room, designed by Andrew Porth Architects.* **ABOVE:** *A Fortuny silk Venetian chandelier is suspended over the formal dining table.*

table. Beyond the patio lies the expansive oak-filled lot to the south of the house. As designed by landscape architect Jodi Holkman and others of Sage Landscape, this inviting space encompasses not only nature but art. A stone pathway weaves through a grove of mature trees, past a white lilac, a reflecting pond, and more flowers; it ends at *A Thinking Man*, a huge bronze sculpture of a seated man by French sculptor Cyrille André. Part of the landscape, as originally conceived by Jones, is the limestone terrace that partially wraps around the southeast corner of the house. It offers an exceptional vantage point, high enough for a view over the parkway and pedestrian path and a glimpse of the glimmering lake that has endured more than a hundred years of development. And the owners remember to notice: "We're never too busy not to realize what a joy it is to live here," they say.

Lake of the Isles Landmarks

PARK BOARD BRIDGE NUMBER 3, LINKING THE ISLES AND CALHOUN
When Lake of the Isles was finally connected to Lake Calhoun, a new bridge was required on Lake Street and Lake of the Isles Parkway. Architects William Cowles and Cecil B. Chapman, Minneapolis, won the park board's design competition in 1911. Their concrete-arch bridge, faced in granite, still works well today.

PEAVEY FOUNTAIN The first public art in Minneapolis's parks was Peavey Fountain, a watering trough for the horses that drew buggies around the lakes and a favored destination for young couples on an evening's ride. Donated by grain miller Frank Peavey in 1891, the fountain still stands as a neighborhood icon at the intersection of Kenwood Parkway and West Lake of the Isles Parkway. Below, the Minneapolis Park Board moves a playful floating sculpture nicknamed "Minne" from lake to lake annually.

KENILWORTH LAGOON In 1912, the wetlands between Cedar Lake and Lake of the Isles were dredged, and the new channel that linked the lakes became known as the Kenilworth Lagoon. Kenilworth Castle in England was the setting for *Kenilworth*, a historical romance by Sir Walter Scott.

Cedar Lake

The park board delayed the acquisition of Cedar Lake for longer than any other lake in the city. In the 1880s, Cedar was far from the city, and other neighborhoods clamored for parks. In 1905 the board acquired enough land to build a parkway on the west shore.

Theodore Wirth, then superintendent of parks, recommended improvements in 1909, including connecting Cedar to Lake of the Isles. Kenilworth Lagoon was excavated in the marshy area between the two lakes, and land around it was built up with dirt from the Isles dredging. When the canal opened, Cedar Lake's water level dropped five feet, creating more shoreline to be used for the parkway. New bridges were then built over the waters linking Isles with Calhoun. On July 5, 1911, a jubilant civic celebration was held as the first boats passed under the bridge. At last the linkage was completed.

The park board continued acquiring land on Cedar, and with a final purchase on the north shore in 1959, the board held nearly all of the property in the city that bordered lakes and rivers.

Long considered the wildest of the chain, Cedar was named for the eastern red cedar trees that lined its shores. It has three sandy beaches and is also popular for canoeing and kayaking. The southeastern shore has remained the one place in the Chain of Lakes where homes are built directly on the shore. These prime building sites feature several modern homes designed by architects, including one of Frank Lloyd Wright's Usonian homes, constructed in 1950, with textured colorful marble on the exterior and interior walls. In general, Cedar Lake's lively housing stock is more contemporary than that of the other lakes, attracting young families, professionals, and retirees as well.

The Peterson House 1960

Designing homes as part of nature has long been a basic concept for Minnesota's modernist architects. For Elizabeth (Lisl) Close, that premise was a vital part of her repertoire. Born in Vienna in 1912 as Elizabeth Scheu, she grew up in a landmark house designed by the avant garde architect Adolph Loos and later brought the European Bauhaus standards to Minnesota, where she married Winston Close. Together they founded their own firm in 1938, Close and Associates, and they created many diverse architectural works over the years. The firm became known for the simplicity and humaneness of its work and especially for designs of custom-made homes throughout the country. Gar Hargens, AIA architect, a member of the design team, became a partner early on and since 1988 has been president and sole owner. In 2002 Elizabeth Close became the first woman to win the AIA Minnesota Gold Medal.

Elizabeth particularly enjoyed her work whenever a lakeside site came up, and in 1959 such an opportunity developed when she was called by Jeanette and Oliver Peterson, parents of four daughters. They owned a large lot of choice property on the eastern shore of Cedar Lake. Jeanette Peterson, whose minor at the University of Minnesota was in architecture, worked closely with Elizabeth on the design. The residence was completed in 1960.

Their Cedar Lake house, built snugly into a partially wooded hillside overlooking the clear blue waters of Cedar, includes a substantial deck that follows the shape of the shoreline. "I like to look out 180 degrees to the point and not see another house," says Oliver Peterson, a retired physician who enjoys playing his organ and piano.

ABOVE: *On the shores of Cedar Lake lies a modernist house designed by Elizabeth Close.* **OPPOSITE:** *The copper hood over the fireplace was instigated by Jeanette Peterson, working with Close.*

The cedar-clad house with brick wainscoting is L shaped, with a long, low, rectangular segment housing the garage and bedrooms at street level; a few steps below is the main level, for a total of three thousand square feet. Instead of a typical flat roof, the structure has a pitched roof with gravel on top.

Stepping into the entry, visitors are greeted with a dazzling view of open water and Cedar Point on the opposite western shore. Down three steps is the great room, a wide-open rectangular space walled with large Pella glass sliding doors facing the view, and on the other side, a brick wall punctuated with grills for distributing the sounds of the built-in organ.

The living room portion features midcentury modern furnishings, beige wool carpeting, and an organ. In the room's center stands a wood-burning fireplace with a handsome hood of copper covering the chimney. This idea was instigated by Mrs. Peterson, who wanted the concrete chimney hidden from view.

A walnut dining table is placed on a cork floor adjacent to the kitchen, with a handy opening tucked into the partial wall between the kitchen and dining area. The neat modern kitchen is square, with ample windows facing south and west and walnut cabinets on the opposite wall. Hanging cabinets and a cooktop range open to a pleasant sun-filled breakfast area.

No change was made in the house until 1970, when the couple retained another modernist, architect John Rauma, to design a small addition at the south end above the ground-floor walkout. This space became the "new" TV and music room, with comfy window seats along the windows facing south and west, bookcases, and shelving for music storage. With four daughters growing up here, the additional fifteen hundred square feet of living space on the ground floor was also well used, for one bedroom, a family room, and storage. The daughters—always in or out on the lake, canoeing, rowing, diving, and sailing—became expert swimmers over the years.

Off the street, the front yard gently slopes to the main level with two walkways, one leading to the main entry door, the other bisecting the lawn and culminating in a sunken small circular concrete and brick seating area. Attractive evergreen plantings are strategically placed to accent the site, with landscaping carried out by landscape architect Jerry Luesse.

Winston Close passed away in 1997, and Elizabeth in 2011. Their legacy includes this timeless modern house, which illustrates how well Close and Associates (with help from these clients) has done in creating flexible yet affordable architecture using natural materials like wood, brick, and concrete. A Close home is one that exudes warmth and hospitality, without formal decorations, one that serves a family well for generations, as exemplified here in the Petersons' inviting 1960s Cedar Lake residence.

ABOVE: *A small addition for use as a library and music room was designed in 1970 by John Rauma, also a modernist.*

OPPOSITE, TOP LEFT: *Original stainless-steel finishes and appliances retain the midcentury modern flavor of the kitchen.* **OPPOSITE, TOP RIGHT:** *Scandinavian furniture complements the wood-paneled pass-through of the dining room.* **OPPOSITE, BOTTOM:** *Modernists were the first to design the now popular "great room," here combining living room and dining areas.*

The Kaufman Lacey House 1936

The International Style first emerged in Minneapolis in 1936, thanks to visionary clients and a young architect, newly graduated from the University of Minnesota with a passion for the new "modern architecture." V. Mel Kaufman and his wife, Henet, were enthusiastic architecture buffs, having visited the Chicago World's Fair in 1933 and studied the works of Richard Neutra. When they heard of a site directly on the shores of sparkling Cedar Lake in Minneapolis, they jumped at the chance to build a home there using what was then the newest style in architecture.

Before selecting an architect, the Kaufmans decided it was imperative to choose someone young enough to have an equal passion for the new look of "less is more." James Brunet, a recent graduate of the University of Minnesota Architecture School and member of the firm Wessel, Brunet & Kline, landed the job. He was delighted, since he had not found any interest among the general public for the International Style. According to Brunet, the home he was about to design would be "one of the first to break away from the popular Colonial and Spanish mode."

The Kaufmans, who had no children, planned a relatively small weekend lakeside retreat, twenty-three hundred square feet of living space in two stories with no basement or attached garage. The Cedar Lake site was exceptional, with a flat lawn dipping gradually to the lakeshore.

The savvy clients insisted on a flat roof and the latest in materials and technology. Accordingly, the architect created an International Style design featuring a ribbon-like stretch of windows reaching across both levels of the house and set into a façade of white stucco. A small narrow

terrace at the south end opened an unexposed view of the lake. Windows were made specifically for the Kaufman house by the Andersen Frame Corporation (now Andersen Corporation) using the new crank-out casements, although they were still the single-pane variety. Translucent glass block both defined the entry and provided privacy on the street façade. Originally, the house's main floor contained a living room, dining room, kitchen, and maid's room; the second floor held three bedrooms and two bathrooms. Although the house was designed to be built of concrete, then the custom in Europe, it was changed to balloon wood framing traditionally used by American home builders.

ABOVE: *The architects carefully set back the new third-floor addition, using the house's 1930s wedding-cake design vocabulary.*
OPPOSITE: *The living room was slightly enlarged using glass block to include a corner for reading.*

The Kaufmans remained in the home until 1979 and were followed by three other owners. In 2001 the Laceys fell in love with the house on first sight soon after they arrived in Minneapolis from Texas. Roger, a 3M executive, and Neroli, a writer, were both English and had lived abroad and traveled extensively. They promptly bought the property, installed modern furnishings, and enjoyed the fun of living at the lake. In 2003, however, their lifestyle changed dramatically with the birth of their first child, a daughter, followed soon by a second little girl. "We were getting quite squeezed for space," said Neroli.

The house had already been designated as a landmark by the Minneapolis Heritage Preservation Commission in 1987, but at the owners' request, the city approved major changes to the home in 1989. The project, designed by Meyer, Scherer & Rockcastle, Ltd. (MS&R), added a family

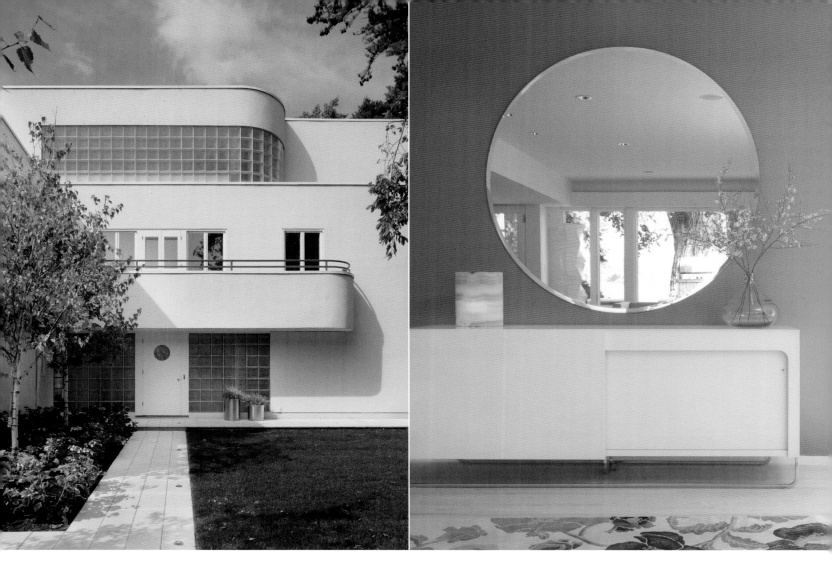

room/office over the garage, expanded existing bathrooms, remodeled the north terrace for storage, installed pipe railings on the existing balconies, and added a spiral stair tower to the new roof terrace. The kitchen floor, with its pattern of three colored triangles, was created and installed by the original owner.

By 2010, the owners felt the house was still too confined. They spent two years looking for a way to expand while staying true to the Neutra philosophy. They also wanted to correct some of the stylistic errors of the previous upgrade. Roger and Neroli then called on Lars Peterssen of Peterssen/Keller Architects to undertake a major renovation. They liked the way Peterssen worked, carefully researching the house history, then delicately improving the home where it needed attention. Fortunately, in the early 1990s the HPC had approved a third-floor addition designed by MS&R that had never been built. Now was the time, the architect said.

It was a significant change. According to Peterssen, "we were determined to maintain the significance of the original design by creating seamless additions that would not compete with the original house." The third-floor addition is a master suite including a bedroom, bathroom, closet, dressing room, and small sitting area with access to a sweeping terrace and broad lake views. Peterssen used glass block and white stucco for the street façade, while he set back the lake side, leaving the original two-story façade intact. The living room was also extended and a small guest room/study with bath was added next to the kitchen, using the design vocabulary of the existing home. While new energy-efficient windows now replace the outmoded single-pane styles, the 2011 retrofit exhibits the same ribbon effect of glass alternating with bands of stucco. Completed in 2011 by builders Streeter and Associates, the home still presents the same International Style expression as the original home of 1936. "This house is a huge box of light," says Neroli.

OPPOSITE, TOP LEFT:

*Another bathroom repre-
sents the updates made by
MS&R Architects, complete
with a mosaic tiled floor
in the spirit of the 1930s.*

OPPOSITE, TOP RIGHT:

*Another peaceful reading
spot in the remodeled
library, opening to the lake.*

OPPOSITE, BOTTOM: *Lars
Peterssen designed this
modern bathroom with
contemporary small glass
tiles as a vanity backsplash.*

ABOVE: *Stairs lead to the
third-floor master suite,
where a great lake view
awaits.*

Entering the gleaming white house via a glass block corridor, one's view is immediately drawn to the lake, so close to this residence. The couple's midcentury modern furnishings are splashed with a joyous color palette of hot pink, bright yellow, and white. Floors are white oak stained blonde. The new white fireplace is set against a wood wall of rift-sawn white oak. A ribbon of windows stretches across the room, bringing the lake view inside. Polished chrome railings now ascend three levels, where bedrooms are painted mostly white, allowing lake vistas to predominate. A lush contemporary bathroom with pale blue tiles is a highlight, while every bedroom in the house now has its own deck. Of all three decks surrounding the house, the best view is from the new third-floor terrace, where you feel like you are on a ship at sea.

Coen+Partners designed the new landscaping, including improved circulation paths and a lengthy front yard garden of blue and purple hydrangeas (Neroli's favorite colored flowers), a cast-concrete paver walkway to the main entry, and a custom-made wood fence on both sides. On the lakeside, a new flat patio and enlarged terrace is placed close to the house where the owners can relax and admire the way the old cottonwood tree frames a view of the lake. With steps down to the lake in their backyard, this family enjoys swimming every day in summers and cross-country skiing across the lake in winters.

As Roger Lacey once described their lake life, "It's as good as the South of France." Neroli adds, "There's nothing like this in New York or London. Cedar is the most beautiful lake I've ever seen, and yet I'm just a few minutes from my office."

The Numero House 1962

Wisconsin architect and Taliesin Fellow James Dresser built a nationwide reputation for creative design in such buildings as the Lake Geneva Public Library, Minnesota's Pavilion at the New York World's Fair, Tommy Bartlett's Robot World, and countless commercial structures, restaurants, and residences. Dresser believed firmly in Wright's principles, which he had learned while apprenticing at Taliesin West and, later, at Spring Green. These were the principles of organic architecture: using natural materials, building within the native environment, and bringing the outdoors in.

Wright was not only his mentor, teacher, and employer; he was also a friend of Dresser's wife's Wisconsin family. Barbara Dresser, the architect's widow, commented, "My father was one of Wright's apprentices and our family felt he was a friend, kind and loving." Throughout her husband's life, his work reflected the master's influence, even though he left the apprenticeship in 1945 to establish his own firm, saying, "I was not interested in becoming an eraser for the master's hand."

One of his numerous clients, who became a lifelong friend, was Joseph Numero, a gifted entrepreneur, co-inventor of the first transport refrigerated control system, and later founder and president of Thermo King Corp., based in Bloomington, Minnesota. Numero liked the way Dresser used the techniques he learned from Frank Lloyd Wright in the homes he designed. In 1962, the architect created a singular one-level home for his client on Cedar Lake Road which he regarded as one of his signature residences. The Numeros enjoyed it for the next twenty-nine years. Following Mrs. Numero's death in 1994, the property was sold to an accountant and his wife, who appreciated the high quality of its design and craftsmanship and highly approved of its advanced heating, cooling, and low-velocity air systems. No one else had ever lived in the house; the buyers found it in impeccable condition and made only minor changes.

What is most striking about this stone-clad house is its exceedingly long low-slung profile protected by a patterned trellis roof with wide eaves. Neighbors say it's the longest roof in the neighborhood. The residence sits directly across the road from Cedar Lake, yet it was obviously designed for privacy. The seven-thousand-square-foot roof covers a five-thousand-square-foot footprint broken up with many windows.

ABOVE: *The approach to this exceptional stone-clad house signals the architectural inspiration of Frank Lloyd Wright.*
OPPOSITE: *The handsome dining room overlooks a landscaped patio.*

Stonework laid by craftsmen encircles the house, broken only by a wall of glass overlooking the backyard landscaping. At the entry, attractive built-in stone planters with greenery, sculptures, a fountain, and a birch tree rising up through the roof greet visitors.

A massive seven-hundred-pound wood door, embellished with a slender wooden frieze, opens into a foyer crafted in travertine marble from Rome. One step down leads to an unusually large living room and entertainment center, complete with a Wright-inspired tall stone fireplace. A unique high ceiling of black walnut with carved wood triangles matches the black walnut paneling in the room with classic Prairie School ornamentation. The architect's design gives the room a

somewhat formal air. In contrast, he also created a 1960s-style circular bar of brown and gold. Wood accordion doors may be used to close off the area. The present owners bought all the elegant furnishings from the original owners, including sofas and chairs made by Dunbar, covered in a soft beige. No wonder they especially enjoy entertaining guests in this unique space.

Other built-ins and custom-made furnishings were also selected by the Numeros. For example, the dining room table and chairs look through a wall of glass into a wide patio and plantings of maple trees, shrub maple, and viburnum. Long halls lead to the bedroom wing (with two bedrooms and baths reminiscent of the 1950s) as well as a comfortable library furnished entirely with leather. A spacious L-shaped kitchen with breakfast and office areas and honey maple cabinets offers a good view of Cedar Lake through the trees.

Although the couple made only minor changes in the house, they made a major improvement—removing all the heavy turquoise and green drapes that had covered every window and replacing them with translucent roman shades. "That brought new life into the house," said the owner. They also replaced most of the matching carpeting. Throughout the house, lighting stands out as one of the architect's major achievements.

Fortunately, the present owners of the Numero house have been longtime admirers of Frank Lloyd Wright and the kind of architecture he represents. After seventeen years of living in what may be called a "cousin" of the famed master's work, they admire the way the late architect James Dresser expressed his deep feelings for the art of architecture and appreciate his influence in their lives.

ABOVE: *A travertine marble floor greets visitors in the elegant foyer.* **OPPOSITE, TOP:** *Modern shelves wrap around a corner near the front entry and lead down a hallway to the master bedroom.* **OPPOSITE, BOTTOM:** *A high ceiling of black walnut with carved wood triangles is an outstanding feature of the living room.*

OPPOSITE, TOP LEFT: *A geometric pattern emerges from the architect's use of wood and stone in the fireplace design.* OPPOSITE, TOP RIGHT: *Dresser's triangular pitched roof is carried out in the patio elevation.* OPPOSITE, BOTTOM LEFT: *The bar's gold foil wallpaper remains intact.* OPPOSITE, BOTTOM RIGHT: *The 1960s television, in a classic cabinet.* RIGHT: *A vintage dressing table.* BELOW: *The L-shaped kitchen includes a breakfast area.*

The Schifman House 2007

You can tell with a glance at architect David Salmela's designs that he is a midwesterner through and through. His work reflects the openness of the prairie skies, the light reflected from Minnesota lakes, the simplicity of rural farmhouses and barns, and the rugged boulders of the North Shore.

Every house, cabin, sauna, lodge, or commercial building he has designed expresses his views of simplicity and living in the natural environment. Of Finnish descent, he conceives the landscape as a powerful focus in his designs. The Duluth architect has received many awards, both national and international, and through it all he has always been an advocate of sustainable design. Thanks to the determination of Minneapolis clients Melissa and James Schifman, he accomplished his first LEED-certified residential design, one that is truly remarkable.

The Schifmans, a young working couple, called him after finding a site across the road from Cedar Lake in the midst of a Minneapolis neighborhood known for less traditional housing. As parents of two young children, they wanted to be close to downtown and yet build a house good for the environment. They chose Salmela after seeing the homes he had designed for Jackson Meadows, the unique community at Marine on St. Croix. As Melissa Rappaport Schifman says, "We wanted a Minnesota architect and I like Salmela's homes because they are connected to the earth."

The couple had located a 1950s rambler on a corner lot across the roadway from Cedar Lake, but after discovering a major mold problem in the basement, they decided it had to be demolished. All wood surfaces and even the appliances were recycled during deconstruction. In 2007, they began

OPPOSITE: Al fresco dining under the cantilevered roof.
RIGHT: Award-winning architect David Salmela designed this contemporary house for sustainability.

working with Salmela with a firm goal of building an energy-efficient home that would win LEED certification. LEED, an acronym for Leadership in Energy and Environmental Design, is a consensus-developed, third-party verified, voluntary rating system that promotes the design and construction of high-performance green homes. The program encompasses site selection, water efficiency, materials and resources, energy, and indoor environmental quality.

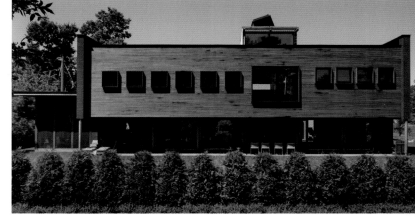

The challenge for the architect was how to provide privacy from the busy roadway, yet open the house to a great view of the sparkling lake beyond, and envelope the structure in sustainability.

Once the soil problems were solved, Streeter and Associates, Inc., built the house in an L shape of reclaimed cypress (from old pickle vats), while both ends of the house were of contrasting materials—natural black brick resembling bookends. The Schifmans decided to keep the cypress oiled because they loved its golden look. The two-level house is light filled with square windows punctuating the lakeside façade separated by a large picture window in the center. The upper level cantilevers over the main floor, where a row of floor-to-ceiling triple-pane windows and double doors lead to a welcoming patio.

The forty-eight-hundred-square-foot residence is sited facing the lake on the east side for morning light and on the west for evening light. Only minimal use of air conditioning is required thanks to the cantilevering sunshades and the ventilating skylight positioned at the highest point of the house where it drives out the hot air. Photovoltaic panels located on the roof of the office provide about 25 percent of the home's electricity from the sun. The main part of the home is connected through a breezeway to the garage, which has an office above for Melissa. The L shape forms a courtyard including an attractive outdoor dining area and a large backyard with play area for the couple's children, as well as two raised-bed vegetable gardens.

Providing privacy along Cedar Shore Drive is an arborvitae hedge bordering a strip of prairie grasses blooming with daisies and yellow coreopsis and adjacent to a field of mowed grass. Green roofs, planted over the entry hall and the garage, feature sedum with red and yellow flowers. The plantings absorb runoff, help insulate the house, and extend the life of the roof.

For the interior, the architect planned a sun porch at the southern end, shaped like a box with black screens, and a great room combining kitchen, dining, seating, TV, and inconspicuous bar. Wood cabinets are fir, walls are white, floors are black slate, and the ceilings are midnight blue. Hanging white globular lights make another architectural statement. Exposed fir beams, sustainably harvested, add contemporary warmth to this open family space. On the north end of the house is an intimate den with small wood-burning fireplace and small alcove for a home office.

PREVIOUS PAGES: *Cooking, eating, television watching, and homework all go on in the great room, which features globular hanging lights, a blue wood-beamed ceiling, and black slate floors.* **ABOVE:** *At the top of the stairs, the family enjoys a parklike view.* **OPPOSITE:** *Hot air rises through the slatted white stairs to the ventilating skylight above.*

An open-tread, reclaimed-fir staircase enclosed in white slatted wood leads upstairs to three square bedroom spaces. Each child has her own colorful space, one with pink walls, the other orange. The Schifmans chose the shady side for their small master bedroom and use an ultra-large bathroom as their dressing room, with his-and-hers wardrobes and individual sinks. In the center of the second floor is a small sitting area, where the family enjoys spectacular views of Cedar Lake.

In general, the house is so light and simple that its playful contemporary design makes living here a joy for this family. Meanwhile, Melissa continues her work as a writer, blogger, and sustainability consultant who helps small businesses save money and natural resources.

In May 2011 the home was awarded LEED Gold certification, the eleventh so designated in Minneapolis. You might say "Go for the Gold" is the motto of the project's team: architect David Salmela; landscape architect Coen+Partners; builder Streeter and Associates; and, in particular, the homeowners, led by Melissa Rappaport Schifman. It is another gold for Salmela, who had already been awarded the AIA Minnesota Gold Medal in 2008 for architectural excellence.

ABOVE: *Light plays a vital role in the architect's design, as in Melissa Schifman's office.* **OPPOSITE, TOP LEFT:** *Not many offices have a green roof out the windows.* **OPPOSITE, TOP RIGHT:** *A screened porch with a high ceiling and a fan provides bug-free outdoor space in the summer.* **OPPOSITE, BOTTOM:** *Salmela provided an unusually large master bathroom, which doubles as dressing room space for the couple.*

ABOVE: *For its overall sustainable design, the house received a LEED Gold rating.* **LEFT:** *Triple-pane windows running floor to ceiling culminate in the ventilating skylight above.* **OPPOSITE, TOP LEFT:** *The skylight is not only functional; it also serves as an aesthetic detail.* **OPPOSITE, TOP RIGHT:** *Photovoltaic panels on the office roof, mounted like awnings, shade the office and provide about 25 percent of the home's electricity. A green roof planted with colorful sedum absorbs runoff and improves insulation.* **OPPOSITE, BOTTOM:** *The L shape forms an ample backyard with picnic and play areas for the family.*

Cedar Lake Landmarks

CEDAR POINT After Cedar Lake was connected to Lake of the Isles, Cedar's level dropped five feet. Louis Island became a peninsula, now known as Cedar Point. Today, this parkland provides a pleasant place to relax, swim, and fish from a pier.

CEDAR LAKE TRAIL The Cedar
Lake Trail, formerly a railroad bed, now
serves bikers, hikers, and joggers.

CEDAR LAKE MAIN BEACH
One of the clearest beaches in the
city is Cedar's main beach, located
at a busy intersection of the parkway.
Clean, quiet, and uncrowded, this
sandy beach is considered one of the
best places to swim in Minneapolis.

Lake Calhoun

The Dakota called this lake either Mdoza (Lake of the Loons) or Mde Maka Ska (Lake of the White Earth), but the whites at Fort Snelling renamed it to honor John Caldwell Calhoun, secretary of war under President Monroe, who had ordered the establishment of the fort. In 1834 the south shore of the lake was the home of a Dakota community headed by Mahpiya Wicasta, or Cloud Man. His people had agreed to learn the whites' way of farming. Gideon and Samuel Pond, brothers and missionaries, built a cabin just east of the lake and began to teach Cloud Man's people to plow and plant. But by 1840, after a change in Indian agents and with rising concerns about recent conflicts with the Ojibwe, the band moved to Oak Grove, now Bloomington.

A few decades later, as the city of Minneapolis grew, this beguiling lake was attracting tourists, nature-lovers, and city dwellers. Because of its sandy beaches, the first public bath house was built in 1890 (for men at first, later for women). By the turn of the century, canoeing and sailing were popular, and the Calhoun Yacht Club was organized in 1901. Calhoun's swampy areas were dredged between 1911 and 1924. The lake's park areas, beaches, and boulevards were all built on man-made land.

The walking, biking, and jogging path around the lake is about three miles in length, and there are three sandy beaches. No wonder so many exceptional neighborhoods were built near the clear blue waters of Lake Calhoun.

The Hillside House 2009

Early in his career, architect Charles Stinson studied with Charles Biederman, a Red Wing artist whose colorful images responded whimsically to the natural world. Stinson also became fascinated with the way Frank Lloyd Wright's compositions reflected their sites' native topography. By the time he founded his own firm, Stinson's design philosophy was firmly rooted in these early influences, and his work became known for its horizontal, vertical, and sometimes curved forms, always reflecting the geography of the site.

Today, with clients in Saudi Arabia, the Caribbean, and across the United States, the Deephaven-based Minnesota architect has built an international reputation for distinguished residential architecture. Through it all, he has never lost his love of drawing and is rarely seen without a trio of colored pencils in his shirt pocket.

One of his latest clients asked him to design a home on a hillside overlooking Lake Calhoun. The team joining him to tackle this challenging project included builder Steven Streeter of Streeter and Associates, Deephaven, interior designer Linda Girvin of Aspen, Colorado, and, of course, the owners.

They devised a clever solution for the hillside. Instead of building a house that would be set into the hill, they created an elevated platform at the rim and set the house, complete with outdoor swimming pool, on top. The hill slopes up about twenty feet from the sidewalk below. Then they encircled the property with a low wall of St. Cloud granite to prevent erosion. On the slope above the public walkway, Shane Coen, landscape architect, said, "We wanted to extend the green buffer that runs along the lake, and strategically placed birch trees, maples, and hardwoods to maximize the views."

The two-story house presents a long, bold image along the rim of the hill where, in closer view, you can see the series of mainly horizontal volumes built of mellow limestone from Mankato, Minnesota. "We all went to Mankato and chose the stone we liked best, then had it cut in slabs so they could be used on the house exactly the way they looked in the ground," says Stinson. The family room, living room, and kitchen overlook a stunning swimming pool that is exactly flush with the patio. The master bedroom suite occupies the west wing, which forms the L of the house. A spectacular view of the Minneapolis skyline appears beyond the treetops.

ABOVE: *Mankato limestone clads this contemporary hillside house designed by Charles Stinson.* **OPPOSITE:** *The sleek, contemporary kitchen integrates stainless steel, marble, striped walnut, and pigment lacquer in stone gray.*

The house feels more compact inside than it appears from the exterior. A tall vertical glass stair tower breaks the horizontal look. One of the main features of this very modern family home is the use of wood, adding warmth and a feeling of comfort. Spalted maple floors are prominent throughout, while many interior walls are paneled in anigre, a tan African wood. Teak soffits are used for the exterior in both windows and doors. Alongside the stone walls facing the pool, several columns were cast in bronze, used inside and out, adding versatility to the façade. In a unique touch from the architect, the glass tower casts light down two stories to a teak-lined powder room with a hand-cast glass sink.

For interior design throughout, the owners chose a friend and artist from Aspen, Colorado, Linda Girvin of River Studio Interiors. According to Girvin, "We tried to balance the organic with the geometric design of the house, bringing organic nature into the hardness of the materials."

Entering the house, visitors pass by an intriguing curved wall and recessed ceiling of Venetian plaster, an architectural composition that helps define the spaces in several other rooms. For the living room, featuring custom-made furnishings and contemporary art, the designer chose soft shades of browns, beiges, and grays, with accents of blue and gold, and a pewter surround and hearth for the fireplace. Lined with anigre wood walls, glass, and soft white "wintertree" draperies, the room allows visitors open vistas of the shimmering lake beyond and the inviting blue pool close by. A singular bar and wine cabinet are built into an adjoining space.

The dining room is located away from the water features but conveniently next to the kitchen and overlooks green space adjoining the family porch. The table, a large slab of darkly stained oak, dominates the room and accommodates ten people. A stone ledge at the window sills, backed by bronze-splattered white silk draperies, serves as the buffet.

The kitchen and family room, always the heart of any home, houses an extra-long bench and breakfast table overlooking the pool and an area for reading, viewing television, and relaxing. For this space, the designer chose a sophisticated color palette of rust, black, and white featuring an off-white sofa, two modern chairs upholstered in rust, an upbeat coffee table of abstract design, and a television with rust metal surround. Curving shelves hold books and other art objects.

Girvin also led the design for the kitchen in collaboration with Mary Jane Pappas of Pappas Design and Ruth Johnson of Charles R. Stinson Architects. Cabinetry by the elite German cabinetmaker

PREVIOUS PAGES: *Showing the latest in contemporary design, the living room features custom-made chandeliers by Jack Kearney and original art on the teak fireplace wall.* ABOVE: *A Charles Stinson design hallmark: a lap-size pool next to a horizontally shaped house lined with walls of glass.* OPPOSITE, TOP LEFT: *A Motherwell print hangs on a teak wall of the entryway.* OPPOSITE, TOP RIGHT: *A small plaster figure greets visitors entering the house.* OPPOSITE, BOTTOM LEFT AND BOTTOM RIGHT: *A Dirade "Out-In" chair takes a commanding space in the futuristic powder room, where a hand-cast glass sink by Peter David Studio of Seattle stands out.*

OPPOSITE, TOP LEFT: *The modern yet rustic dining table under a chandelier by Aqua Creations.* **OPPOSITE, TOP RIGHT:** *Shelving in the family room provides an artful focal point for ceramics, prints, and books.* **OPPOSITE, BOTTOM:** *The lead interior designer, Linda Girvin, created a comfortable yet sophisticated family room adjoining the kitchen.* **ABOVE:** *From the green rooftop, the owners can see the Minneapolis skyline across Lake Calhoun.*

Bulthaup, specified by the owners, features horizontally striped walnut and aluminum gray facing. In addition, all countertops, the kitchen island, and the backsplash are of beautiful white marble with gold vein. A pewter counter for casual meals projects out from the island, which is flanked by a walk-in pantry.

Sustainability was also a key design element for the owners and architect. Underneath the granite auto court are forty geothermal wells, which heat the interior and the pool. A green roof, made up of sedums and grasses, is another environment-friendly attribute. The tower features two kinds of solar glass, one partially transparent and the other partially obscure. In addition, the stairs are built of reclaimed wood. Building materials were obtained locally, as much as possible, according to builder Steven Streeter.

The family has occupied this Minneapolis lake home since its completion in 2009 and is still finding new ways to enjoy the space, exploring the private roof deck, playing croquet in the side yard, having casual cookouts, inviting friends for fun events, and especially plunging into their own pool high above the lake. "We love living in an active, urban environment," say the owners, and Stinson's stunning design delivers what they planned.

Cottage City
1883–2012

Even in the late nineteenth and early twentieth centuries, lakeshore homes were not affordable for working-class Minneapolitans. On the south shore of Lake Calhoun, however, a new neighborhood known as Cottage City sprang up after 1883, featuring little clapboard cottages built on tiny twenty-five-foot-wide lots. The houses were economical to build, they could serve a family well—and they were close to the lake. In these early years, building sites extended from the natural lakeshore directly up steep hills overlooking the lake. Today's Calhoun Parkway was placed on fill from lake dredging in the 1920s.

According to architect and community historian Peter Sussman, the compact neighborhood was a marketing concept of developer Louis Menage, who bought and platted the property reaching from Lake Calhoun south to Fortieth Street and west from Richfield Road to Xerxes Avenue. The area is still known as Cottage City, befitting the small size and simplicity of the homes. The Lyndale Railroad "Motor Lane," which reached Lake Harriet in 1880, provided access to town. In the construction boom after World War II, people built on marginal lots, replaced existing homes, and generally upgraded housing in the area. The homes that survive from those earliest days can be seen in updated condition on streets ranging from Thomas and Sheridan to Upton and Vincent. All together, the cottages are recognized as part of Linden Hills.

ABOVE, OPPOSITE, AND FOLLOWING PAGES:

Turn-of-the-century cottages in this compact neighborhood. Some were built as summer homes, others for year-round living, and some were newly designed to fit in with the old cottages.

Few architects were involved with the earliest homes; more often, local carpenters and builders designed and built these engaging cottages, adding their own ingenuity and producing homes of real charm. Architectural styles varied from Dutch to Colonial, Swiss to Cape Cod.

One of the most unusual designs is a log cabin or cottage of vertical logs built in 1900 by Charles and Mattie Mousseau, who found a prize site high above the lake. It has survived the years, set within a complex of two other houses, and now sports a new addition, modern siding, and a hip roof.

The oldest surviving Cottage City home is a clapboard-sided vernacular farmhouse, built for Mary Copley in 1883. Originally built at Thirty-ninth and Sheridan South, it has been moved to Glendale Terrace. The twin Chadwick Cottages on Fortieth Street, built in 1902 as side-by-side carpenter cottages, were connected by an addition in 1972, forming a charming home for the present owners. An outstanding example of craftsmanship is the Swiss Chalet–style house on Fortieth Street, designed by Lowell A. Lamoreaux, exhibiting a traditionally carved wood façade and chalet-style roof. Sited well back on their Thomas Avenue South lots are three of the original twenty-five-foot-wide cottages, each painted a different color but each with a distinctive flair, a screened porch, and overflowing gardens in front. Most are trimmed in white. Despite a century of changes and remodels, these little cottages are still a delight.

The homes are not protected from development, so many are being torn down and replaced. But with renewed interest in historic neighborhoods, local preservationists and homeowners may work to save a vital part of the city's architectural heritage.

Lake Calhoun Landmarks

THE BAKKEN LIBRARY AND MUSEUM *3537 Zenith Avenue South* A lavish seventeen-room mansion was built in 1930 for William Goodfellow, who had sold his dry goods store to George Dayton and made a fortune. The Tudor Revival house, West Winds, was designed by architect Carl Gage, who used half timbering over stucco and stone for the exterior and enriched the interior with dark wood paneling, intricate wood carving, a great hall, and grandly sized rooms. Set well back from Lake Calhoun, the estate has an excellent lake view, with handsomely landscaped grounds designed by landscape architect Michael Swingley. Two other owners occupied the house until 1976, when Medtronic founder Earl Bakken purchased it and established the Bakken Museum, donating his library and his collection of antique medical-electrical devices. In 1998, Meyer, Scherer & Rockcastle, Ltd., designed a large expansion, doubling the building's size but retaining many of the original historic rooms and its 1930s style.

CALHOUN BEACH CLUB *2925 Dean Parkway*
Construction began in 1928 on the Calhoun Beach Club, a luxury club and apartment building designed by Chicago architect Charles M. Nichol in the Renaissance Revival style. Unfortunately for its investors, the disruptions of the Great Depression and World War II caused this popular Minneapolis landmark to stand unfinished from 1929 until 1946. It has been operated as a social club, a hotel, apartments, and a home for the elderly. In 2002, the building was extensively renovated as the Vintage Apartments, which include a health club, retail spaces, meeting rooms, and a ballroom.

THE MINIKAHDA COUNTRY CLUB *3205 Excelsior Boulevard*
Founded in 1898, the Minikahda Country Club is the oldest golf course west of the Mississippi. Perched on top of the bluff west of Lake Calhoun, the club's site was chosen by community leaders Thomas Lowry, William Dunwiddie, and Andreas Ueland. The Minikahda clubhouse was designed in the Greek Revival style by Long and Long in 1899. In the years since, the clubhouse has undergone numerous additions and renovations and remains a popular social and golfing destination.

LAKEWOOD MEMORIAL CHAPEL Harry Wild Jones's shining example of Byzantine architecture, modeled after the Hagia Sophia in Istanbul, Turkey, was completed in 1910. New York designer Charles Lamb created the stunning mosaic interior.

THE LAKEWOOD CEMETERY GARDEN MAUSOLEUM When the Lakewood Cemetery Association decided another mausoleum was needed, its board awarded the commission in 2009 to HGA Architects and Engineers, with Joan Soranno as designer. Her minimalist architecture embraces the cemetery's pastoral landscape and legacy. Clad in rough-textured gray granite and white mosaic marble, the two-level structure quietly encompasses options for cremation and crypt entombment and offers areas for contemplative family experiences. It was dedicated in January 2012.

Lake Harriet

Beautiful Lake Harriet was named for Harriet Lovejoy, wife of the commandant at Fort Snelling, in 1819. Originally, the Dakota called the lake Mde Uŋma or Other Lake. By the 1880s, the lake and land around it were part of a fourteen-hundred-acre farm owned by Colonel William S. King, one of the founders of the Minneapolis Park Board. He donated the land to the city in 1885 with other property that became Lakewood Cemetery; the donation set a precedent that was largely followed for later parks.

The acquisition of Lake Harriet was the first large project for the new Board of Park Commissioners, a major priority they addressed after first establishing neighborhood parks throughout the city. They built a dirt road around the lake in 1885–86, thus making it the first city lake to boast a parkway.

When Thomas Lowry's streetcar line, the Twin City Rapid Transit Company, reached the lake, its recreational use and its population began to grow. In 1888, to increase traffic, the company built a pavilion on fill added to the north shore where it offered concerts, but the structure was destroyed by fire in 1891. The next two pavilions were designed by the popular architect Harry Wild Jones, but again natural calamities destroyed each one. The city erected yet another pavilion in 1917, which remained standing until 1985, when it was replaced by the current structure, designed by Milo Thompson. Music has always played a vital role at Lake Harriet.

Lake Harriet is the second-largest lake in the Chain of Lakes. True to the city's early visionaries' predictions, many stately homes were built on the parkway from 1910 to the 1930s. They include Tudor Revival styles, as well as Mediterranean, Classical, Colonial, Normandy, and Modern.

The LeJeune Morgan House 1996

Tom Ellison, well-known Minneapolis architect and founder of TEA2 Architects, Inc., feels strongly about substance and integrity in his firm's designs of traditional architecture. He believes in bringing innovative materials and concepts into his firm's work, resulting in high-quality, beautiful homes for contemporary living.

Dan Nepp, Ellison's partner, expressed those beliefs in his design for Jean and Larry LeJeune's house on Lake Harriet Boulevard, completed in 1996. The LeJeunes wanted a new house in a good neighborhood and one with a view. Fortunately, they found a wonderful location on the southwestern curve of the road. It turned out to be the last empty lot left on the lake, formed on what had been the garden of a neighboring historic home. But there was one drawback—it was exceedingly narrow, only fifty-six feet wide. And the program called for a five-thousand-square-foot house, including basement. The architects' goal was to create a substantial home, like others around the lake, but one with a cool lakeside air.

They devised two ways to maneuver the new abode into its site, maintain its privacy, and still build it to fit into the neighborhood full of high-grade, well-settled homes. One way was to shrink the width of the second floor and position it asymmetrically to reduce the scale of the house and give it a "sweeping profile"—thus keeping it in form and rhythm with the neighbors and adding lake views. The other was to give the house a side entrance. According to Nepp, this allowed the main rooms to be shaped as needed, so they could open directly to a raised terrace and lake view without a bisecting front walk.

In 2005, Sheila Morgan, an independent arts advocate, bought the house, making sure there was enough room for her seven grandchildren to play in the basement recreation room. She loves the light that pours into this sophisticated house. "I've never had so much light, and so much open space," she says.

The architects began with a large overhanging roof of red cedar shingles (which have darkened naturally over fifteen years) and clad the house in a light creamy stucco with olive green trim. The roof design is one of the outstanding features that gives this home its character. Actually, there are two roofs, one steeper pitched on top with a slightly curving flair over a lower pitched roof at the first floor so they seem to flow together.

Because the main entry is at the side of the house along the driveway, the main-floor rooms could be placed toward the lake. As Morgan says, "When you enter here, you have no idea of how the rest of the house opens up to the lake—until you turn the corner." The main idea here is discovery, as Ellison would say. The owner enjoys the house just as it is and has made little change beyond a few wallpaper selections upstairs.

In fact, as you enter the living room, your eye immediately goes to the lake vista. This spacious room, designed by Carol Belz, interior designer, has a relatively high ceiling (slightly over eleven feet) and is attractively furnished in Morgan's favorite colors of aqua and cream, set against faux-painted cream-colored walls. Since art plays a big part in the owner's life, she is pleased to

ABOVE: *Architect Dan Nepp, TEA2 partner, devised space for a patio in front of this home and a deck on top, protected by one of the cedar-shingled roofs.*
OPPOSITE: *A cozy corner faces the lake.*

LEFT: *The owners' taste for art is shown in this symmetrical seating area.*
BELOW: *By designing the main entry on the side elevation, the result is ample space for the living room to face Lake Harriet.*
OPPOSITE: *A dramatic two-story entry and stairway with traditional wrought-iron railing. Because the home's design places the main entry on the side elevation, the living room can face Lake Harriet.*

have enough wall space to hang some of her favorite paintings. The room looks out to a small semicircular terrace screened from the parkway by a low hedge and partially shaded by the overhanging roof.

Adjoining the living room, a row of clerestory windows overlooks a sleek island kitchen. A small dining area next to the front windows was carefully placed to take advantage of open sky and good views of the lake to the east and northeast.

Upstairs, Sheila has redecorated the master bedroom, choosing a feminine light blue and white color scheme for the walls, bedspread, and chaise lounge. A row of seven smaller windows facing north brings in light. The basement, remodeled primarily as a place for her grandchildren to play, features an extra-large red couch, a large-screen television, and two guest bedrooms.

To live on this popular lake would be a dream come true for many people. Where else can you swim, sail, hear concerts, eat popcorn, jog or walk, and improve your health at the same time? They say Lake Harriet has it all. And Sheila Morgan appreciates life every day from her "traditional" yet modern house.

ABOVE: *Finished in warm-toned European beech, the kitchen has work areas cleverly hidden from the adjoining living room by a low wood wall.* **OPPOSITE, TOP LEFT:** *A hand-painted bureau doubles as the vanity in the powder room.* **OPPOSITE, TOP RIGHT:** *The main dining area, placed adjacent to the kitchen, overlooks Lake Harriet Parkway.* **OPPOSITE, BOTTOM LEFT:** *Clerestory windows bring natural light into the workable galley kitchen.* **OPPOSITE, BOTTOM RIGHT:** *A wrought-iron railing surrounds the stairs ascending from the foyer.*

The Walling Russell House 1930

In the 1920s, the Tudor Revival style of architecture was spreading rapidly throughout American suburbs and cities. According to many, its five centuries of history, mainly from Britain, projected the feeling of "home." For Minneapolis realtor Benjamin B. Walling, this is exactly what he wanted for his own new home. He knew just whom to call: Minnesota architect Gottlieb Magney, of Magney and Tusler, the firm that had designed the Foshay Tower and many period revival residences.

Magney created an 1890s English cottage version of Tudor Revival, without the half timbering but with three sharply peaked roofs and a handsome rustic coursed brick façade, obviously laid by experienced craftsmen. Wood-framed windows look out over a long lawn to the shores of Lake Harriet, where the house was built on a corner lot along Russell Avenue. The 5,038-square-foot house was completed in 1930, and the Minneapolis Heritage Preservation Commission gave it landmark designation in 1987.

After Walling, another owner purchased the house in the mid- to late 1990s. By 2007, along came the third buyer, another commercial real estate professional, Todd Russell, who had just moved back to Minnesota from California and was looking for the right house. "I wanted to find a home rich in Minnesota history with architecture reflecting the same. That perfect residence was found here along the shores of Lake Harriet," he said. The home's beautiful views of Lake Harriet also appealed to Russell.

After moving in, Russell immediately began restoring the home's exterior, replacing the slate and copper roofs and gables as well as the gutters and downspouts. The slate had served for eighty years and was well worn. The various pitch of the roofs and the complexity of the three sloping roofs coming together created a challenging task. Russell spent significant time consulting with a professional on selecting the new slate colors, as it was important to him to match the original roof. The new slate roof should serve well for another eighty to one hundred years. He also replaced the exterior wood surrounding the lead windows, which had rotted.

The asymmetrical house bears a Tudor Revival arched entry, framed in wood, with a built-in settee and powder room on either side of the entryway, which leads into a foyer with central staircase and wrought-iron railing. Down two steps is a long, slender living room, pleasantly arranged with furnishings befitting the period and a row of leaded-glass windows offering views of Lake Harriet. Mahogany-beamed ceilings and significant wood trim help give the room the feeling of luxury and comfort often found in this architectural style. Atop the fireplace hangs a rifle, as though this could be a gentleman's lodge.

To the right of the entry is a pleasant dining room with outstanding leaded-glass windows overlooking the lake and an adjoining kitchen. Although the kitchen was spacious enough, Russell felt it did not project the feeling of the period, so he had it remodeled, re-creating moldings and trim as seen throughout the house.

ABOVE: *Gottlieb Magney designed this handsome English cottage version of Tudor Revival.* **OPPOSITE:** *In the rectangular living room, tall wood-framed windows offer splendid views of Lake Harriet.*

Upstairs, the master bedroom, decorated in masculine tones, boasts a fireplace, mahogany-beamed ceilings, and appropriate dressing rooms. Original sailing paintings and photographs abound in this area. The upper south wing of the house, which was once the servants' quarters, is being redesigned to accommodate additional guest suites.

A cozy wood-paneled library overlooks the southern exposure of the home, where Russell has redone the outdoor entertainment area and gardens. Craftsmen have created a fireplace that reflects the high quality of the home's architecture. The bricks for this project, sourced in upstate New York, match the house perfectly—a rare achievement.

When Russell first saw the Walling house, it was covered with ivy, which he has either redirected or removed to expose more of the handsome brick. He has also re-landscaped the entire property. Mature native trees add to the grace and status of his home.

It's interesting to consider what Magney, the original architect, would think about this home's latest owner, a man dedicated to preserving the structure's original character. Todd Russell is one real estate developer who really knew what he was looking for and what to do when he found it.

ABOVE: *The patio with custom-designed hearth echoes the brick pattern from the front door.* **LEFT:** *A fireplace embellished with intricately carved wood warms the master bedroom.* **OPPOSITE, TOP LEFT:** *The stairway makes a stunning curve as it reaches toward the second floor.* **OPPOSITE, TOP RIGHT:** *An outstanding leaded-glass window brightens the bench seating in the entryway.* **OPPOSITE, BOTTOM LEFT:** *The massive front door has elements of English Tudor tradition: hobnails, raised paneling, and a peek-through window.* **OPPOSITE, BOTTOM RIGHT:** *The owner has also re-landscaped the entire property.*

The Madsen Fiterman House 1923

To enter Dolly Fiterman's Mediterranean-style villa is like walking into a land of enchantment projected by world-famous artists whose works hang in every room of her house. For the vivacious Dolly, now retired from her University Avenue gallery known to every art-lover in Minneapolis, "It's a wonderful feeling to see the artists I've collected for years and now to see them in my own rooms." Her collection includes such internationally renowned names as Andy Warhol, Jim Dine, Milton Avery, and Walter de Kooning.

The Fiterman home, built for M. C. Madsen in 1923 on Lake Harriet Parkway, expresses the Spanish Revival period of architecture popular in the 1920s, complete with brilliant white stucco façade and red tile roof. Charcoal wrought-iron trim outlines the arched leaded-glass windows and lines the railing of the terrace, which offers a panoramic view of the lake. At the street entrance, on red pedestals next to the steps, Dolly added four white concrete globes descending in size. Other tall abstract sculptures placed on the lawn sloping toward the lake denote that an art-lover lives here.

The original architect, Albert Van Dyck, who had been an associate of Harry Wild Jones, is known only for several homes that he designed, including the Harry A. Bullis residence on Lake of the Isles. Edward Fiterman, Minneapolis financier, bought the property in 1938, married Dolly Janssen in 1957, and died in 1984. Dolly brought art into his life and later opened her own art gallery in the former Pillsbury Branch Library, a classic building of white marble on University and Central avenues. "My goal was to have a high-quality gallery on a par with the East Coast and give exposure to young talent." Through her work, which involved many trips to New York and Europe, Dolly became well acquainted with many of the famous artists of the 1960s.

ABOVE: *After the well-known art dealer Dolly Fiterman retired from her popular gallery, she built a large modern addition onto her white stucco Mediterranean villa to house her art collection.* **OPPOSITE:** *Anne Loch's painting of two roses includes both realistic and, further to the right, abstract versions.*

After her husband's death and her later retirement from the gallery, she decided the house needed an addition, to include plentiful wall space for large paintings and a swimming pool and spa as well. Dae Min, a Korean native practicing architecture in Minneapolis, was commissioned to design it. The result, completed in the late 1980s, was an ultramodern atrium, thirty-five-hundred square feet in size, with a twenty-five-foot ceiling finished in wood. A surprising element is a lap-size swimming pool, encased in an elongated bright red tube, that stretches three stories above the atrium. Spa facilities complete the scene. Entering the house from the new lavender-colored back door into a plush sitting room with marble floor and looking up at walls of art and the pool, visitors can't help exclaiming, "Wow!" Despite its modern expression, the addition serves as an enhancement to the original architecture.

The main entrance to the house is at the side under a portico and granite terrace. Two pink marble lions greet visitors entering through double doors decorated with an abstract wrought-iron design. This newer foyer with marble floors (and its whimsical sculptural setting) also opens to the atrium; two steps lead up to the original living room, where Andy Warhol's *The Birth of Venus* hangs above the fireplace. Traditionally furnished, this room offers the best views

of Lake Harriet through a series of French doors, outlined in wrought iron, opening to the terrace. In one corner hang works by one of Dolly's favorite artists, Milton Avery. In the adjoining dining room, guests can marvel at paintings by Juan Miro, Marc Chagall, and Minnesota's own Charles Biederman.

The atrium's large walls feature a pair of huge works by Anne Loch, one showing one red and one yellow rose, and the other an abstract version of the first. Looking directly into the atrium is a dramatic painting by Gilbert & George, titled *Eyed*. Dolly tells of a solo trip she took to Moscow for an exhibition of their works where the local art press called her "a personification of American ebullience."

Now enjoying her retirement years as she relaxes in the cozy TV corner of her atrium, Dolly reflects how happy and contented she feels surrounded by her artists. When she glances around this room, she sees a Louise Nevelson sculpture, a de Kooning painting, a Picasso pencil drawing, and a James Rosenquist, among others. Laughingly she recalls the words of the art critic Donald Kuspet, who had visited her dazzling home and then said, overcome by what he had seen, "My pen doesn't write any more."

PREVIOUS PAGES: *Artworks by famous contemporary painters line every wall of the home's large-scale atrium.* **ABOVE:** *Louise Nevelson sculptures flank the entry hall of the atrium.*
OPPOSITE, TOP LEFT: *Ti Shan Hsu's yellow acrylic multimedia work* Compressed Expression, *1986.* **OPPOSITE, TOP RIGHT:** *The double doors of the side entrance, embellished with a wrought-iron screen, welcome visitors under a portico and granite terrace.*
OPPOSITE, BOTTOM LEFT: *The painting* Eyed, *by Gilbert and George, 1984.*
OPPOSITE, BOTTOM RIGHT: *Modern art stands in contrast to the traditional wing.*

OPPOSITE: *White concrete globes placed on red pedestals mark the front steps.* **ABOVE LEFT:** *The dining room holds a painting by Minnesota artist Charles Biederman—and many others.* **ABOVE RIGHT:** *The photo of a lady in white is Michelangelo Pestoletto's Speeachio, a serigraph collage on stainless steel, 1984.* **RIGHT:** *Andy Warhol's painting* The Birth of Venus *hangs over the living room fireplace.*

The Rand McGlynn-Phelps House, 1915

The stately Beaux-Arts mansion known as the Rand house, with its flat roof crowned by balustrades and inset windows, casts a renewed elegance over Lake Harriet Parkway thanks to an extensive four-year restoration by its current owners, Nancy McGlynn Phelps and James Phelps. The taupe stucco exterior and pale green trim framing the windows command a sweep of spring green lawn and lush perennial gardens.

Designed by Minnesota architect Ernest Kennedy, the house demonstrates his prowess with the European classicism that young architects of the era so admired. Although he attended the University of Minnesota, he continued his studies at the Sorbonne in Paris, then returned to Minneapolis to open his own firm specializing in high-end residential architecture.

Among his best-known clients was Rufus R. Rand, whose family was the principal shareholder of the Minneapolis Gas Company. Construction was completed in 1915. Rand's son, Rufus Jr., built the Rand Tower (1929) in Minneapolis and a mansion (1930–31) on Lake Minnetonka that later became the headquarters of Cargill, Inc.

Following World War II, the Rand mansion was divided into a duplex, first occupied by MBA graduate students working at General Mills, then by the Jesuit community, and finally by the Church Universal and Triumphant. The church installed over forty residents, subdivided the great rooms, neglected maintenance, and ultimately moved out in 1989.

OPPOSITE: The home's restored dining room, lighted by a suspended Italianate skylight, features an etched-glass railing inspired by Paul Manship's The Four Elements.

RIGHT: Imbued with European classicism, Minnesota native Ernest Kennedy designed this Beaux Arts mansion for the Rand family. Nancy McGlynn Phelps and James Phelps undertook a four-year restoration to revive the structure's original beauty.

The restoration expert Elizabeth Hyatt then bought the house and began the painstaking task of transformation. She re-created all the doors and millwork, replaced the windows, installed a modern kitchen, improved the grade and drainage, and erected a handsome stucco wall and wrought-iron fence around the property. Hyatt's crew even lifted and structurally supported the marble staircase, which had sunk one and a half inches below

the marble baseboards. They also opened up the ceiling of the first-floor dining room and replaced the second-floor skylight, thereby bringing natural light into the space. Hyatt sold the house in 1992 to new owners, the Sabes, who subsequently sold to the Moores.

By 1999, the McGlynn Phelpses were searching for an architecturally significant city lakes home suitable for their art collection. Captivated by the location, the light, and the layout, the couple purchased the Rand residence. They were intent on preserving its architectural integrity while updating its systems. With considerable education in the arts, their goal was to use their artwork and carefully crafted focal points in each room to enliven Kennedy's vision. Lighting designer Michael Cohen of Schuler Shook enhanced these focal points. Architect Ron Betcher of Oertel Architects, Inc., was commissioned as project architect for the restoration.

On arrival, visitors step up into an elegant elliptical-shaped foyer with a white marble floor and curved blue-green perimeter. Pale aqua-tinted walls reaching up to a twenty-six-foot ceiling are

OPPOSITE, TOP LEFT: *A dramatic marble stairway leads up to the second level, which houses a library, five bedrooms, and the upper media room.* OPPOSITE, TOP RIGHT: *A classic Italianate chair is part of a small conversation area in the living room.*

OPPOSITE, BOTTOM LEFT: *In the grand foyer, a réplique of* Automedon with the Horses of Achilles *by Henri Regnault stands out.*

OPPOSITE, BOTTOM RIGHT: *The graceful wrought-iron railing by acclaimed ironworker Josef Bernasek.*

ABOVE: *The stunning, elliptically shaped foyer with white marble floor and stairway.*

lined with artworks from the sixteenth through the nineteenth centuries. Silk damask draperies of the same hues frame the dramatic two-story stairway window. The marble staircase is noteworthy for its graceful handcrafted wrought-iron railing created by Josef Bernasek, the acclaimed ironworker whose national commissions include the U.S. Senate building in Washington, DC, the Salt Lake (Mormon) Tabernacle in Utah, and the Foshay Tower gates in Minneapolis.

The solarium, originally a summer entrance, is appropriately placed along the sweeping curve of the long southwest wall. Tall windows and French doors frame the rose garden beyond. The herringbone-patterned paduak wood floor is bordered with an elaborate geometric design. The owners created a stairway to the gardens and re-hung the original Rand alabaster chandelier in the solarium.

The most stunning room in the house is the dining room. The thirty-foot ceiling and etched-glass railing of the second-floor balcony are works of art. During the renovation, the McGlynn Phelpses opened the roof, installed a carefully engineered structural skylight, and created beneath it a suspended Italianate art skylight inspired by the Walter Library at the University of Minnesota. The formerly rectangular opening was modified to reflect the rounded corner columns of the atrium. On the etched-glass railing, Glass Art Design re-created *The Four Elements* by Paul Manship, the famous Minnesota sculptor noted for his *Prometheus* at Rockefeller Center, New York.

Facing the sparkling western vista of Lake Harriet, the living room is saturated with color—golds, corals, reds, and blues, orchestrated throughout by interior designer Sandra Mangel.

PREVIOUS PAGES: *Nancy McGlynn Phelps, who loves color, planned these bright coral sofas and handsome damask draperies for the living room.* OPPOSITE, TOP LEFT: *Dining room detail.* OPPOSITE, TOP RIGHT: *A Chinese screen with inset cloisonné panels sets off a Baltic red–striped chair in the living room.* OPPOSITE, BOTTOM LEFT: *A grand piano in the living room.* OPPOSITE, BOTTOM RIGHT: *A portrait of Sarah Bernhardt by Theobald Chartran highlights the deep blue dining room wall.* ABOVE: *Sumptuous crimson, burgundy, and burnished gold fabrics encase the family room, with re-created Honduran mahogany woodwork.*

Decorative crown moldings, a grand piano, and paintings by Frederick Lord Leighton and Paul Oxborough complete the formal scene.

The family room and informal dining room, which stretches along the south side of the home's first floor, was originally the Rands' dining room and breakfast room. Completely furnished in crimson, this room glows with re-created mahogany Honduran woodwork, burnished gold window treatments, and antique French chandeliers.

In the restored kitchen, three Murano glass light fixtures hang over the center island while caramel-colored granite clads the work surfaces and forms the backsplashes. Diaspro marble inserts appear like paintings behind the cooktop and beneath the lighted china cabinets. A cozy window seat overlooking the south gardens adds warmth to the breakfast area.

The second floor houses five bedrooms, each with its own bathroom, an upper solarium overlooking the lake and gardens below, and a spacious theater with views of the atrium's glass panels and the entrance hall's two-story window. An upstairs library with paduak cabinetry and intricate floor designs was created by the designers and owners.

Landscape architecture designed by Joseph Favour of Oslund Landscape Architects and Ron Betcher has also played a prominent part in this restoration. In a neighborhood of Tudor revivals and other styles, the Rand/McGlynn-Phelps house stands out as a jewel of the lakes on its corner site with its handsome wrought-iron gates, railings, and arbors surrounding the property.

This is the home of a couple who recognized the classic beauty of a design worth preserving, committed four years of thoughtful and meticulous restoration to it, and found a sensitive way to add to its beauty. Rufus Rand would be amazed.

Lake Harriet Landmarks

LAKE HARRIET BAND SHELL AND REFECTORY Milo Thompson, a Minneapolis architect at Bentz/Thompson/Rietow, Inc., rewarded the public with his playful, fanciful, yet modern band shell framing the shores of Lake Harriet. Built in 1986 where three former pavilions were once sited, the structure rises to a great arch over a metal truss flanked by two picturesque towers. Music fans gather in front of the band shell's stage for concerts every summer. After the program they wander to the neighboring Refectory, a small takeout eatery set in a fun-filled fantasy-like castle complete with six medieval-style towers. In 1990 Thompson was awarded a national American Institute of Architects award for his band shell achievement.

WILLIAM BERRY PARK *(including the Rose Garden and Lyndale Park Peace Garden)*
The Lake Harriet Rose Garden may be the most beloved garden in Minneapolis. Initiated
in 1907 by the indefatigable park superintendent Theodore Wirth, it is, in fact, located in
William Berry Park, originally Interlachen Park, renamed in honor of the city's first park
superintendent, William Berry, in 1916. The Peace Garden was built as a rock garden in
1929 but was forgotten from the 1940s until 1981, when a tornado uncovered its remains.
Restoration work began, and in 1998 it was rededicated as the Lyndale Park Peace Garden,
containing stones from the cities of Hiroshima and Nagasaki among the flowers.

ELF HOUSE Children leave written wishes for the elf who reportedly lives at the base
of this tree on the south side of Lake Harriet.

Acknowledgments

I wish to thank my collaborator and partner Bette Hammel for her hard work and determination in co-producing this book with me. Her vision, drive, tenacity, and strength of spirit inspired me throughout the process. Also, my deepest gratitude goes to her supportive and generous friends whose financial contributions made our journey possible.

The starting point was to research the best and most appropriate houses throughout the four city lakes for their historical and architectural significance. Many sources and people pointed us in the right direction. Larry Millett's book *AIA Guide to the Minneapolis Lake District* was our road map and bible to finding the best lakeside houses, and realtors Barry Berg and Cotty Lowry offered helpful direction and advice on choice houses for interior spaces. Residential historian Bob Glancy provided an extensive listing of his research on the Kenwood area homes.

Many thanks to my crew of assistants: Megs Molnau, Micah Helling-Christy, Sara Kirk, Heather Byington, and Jada Vogt. Also thanks to Jay Bruns and Beth Fellman, who created lovely environments in each room through their styling talents (Barber house styling and staging by Jayne Lemieux). West Photo generously donated rental equipment when needed, and Cyn Bloom, Katie R. Ann, Tim Meegan, and Fifth Street Design supported the production. Thanks to Ellen Huber for her beautiful and inspired book design and to my husband Philip Prowse for his helpful advice and editing expertise in sifting through the thousand-plus images that went into the making of this book.

Special thanks go to the donors who through their generous contributions made the production of the book possible. Also to Jada Hansen of the Hennepin History Museum, who supported our fundraising efforts as our fiscal agent. At the Minnesota Historical Society Press, I wish to thank Pam McClanahan, Ann Regan, Dan Leary, Shannon Pennefeather, and Alison Aten for their support.

Last but not least, my thanks to all the homeowners who graciously opened their doors to the creative process of having their homes documented for the book. I appreciate their hospitality as Bette and I worked to illustrate their houses in the best light, as well as their willingness to share their stories with our readers.

Karen

Following the Minnesota Historical Society Press's publication of our first "Legendary Homes" book, describing homes on Lake Minnetonka, Barbara Flanagan wrote in her *Star Tribune* column, "I hope these ladies will consider doing a similar book about our city's lakes." It didn't take us long to decide. What other city in America has such beautiful lakes so close to downtown with landscaped public roads and trails surrounding them? MHS Press enthusiastically agreed, and I began the research.

I was immediately struck by the historic decisions made by the early leaders of our Minneapolis Park Board, who foresaw the potential of creating a Chain of Lakes where handsome neighborhoods would be bounded by public parkways. For the research that followed, I am eternally grateful to many people, especially writer Larry Millett, author of the AIA *Guide to the Minneapolis Lake District*, without which we could not have created this book. When multitalented photographer Karen Melvin and I began scouting architecturally and historically significant homes, we chose several from his guidebook. Bob Glancy, known as the "Sherlock of Kenwood" with his many historic calendars, was of major help.

Further guidance in selecting the homes came from Linda Mack, Allan Lathrop, Dan Avchen, and other architects. We will always be especially thankful to the homeowners who so graciously opened their homes for us. Through our interviews with them, I learned a great deal of architectural history, and thanks to Karen's knowledge of interior design and her artistic focus on architectural details, I learned even more.

Thanks also go to the Hennepin History Museum, who served as our fiscal agent, and for the steadfast support of Executive Director Jada Hansen, her staff, and archivist Susan Larson-Fleming. Our generous donors helped make this book possible. We can't thank them enough.

Other major research was carried out downtown at the Minneapolis Collection in the Hennepin County Library, where Ian Stade was extremely helpful.

Most of all, I thank my editor, Ann Regan, Editor in Chief of the Minnesota Historical Society Press, for substantially improving my writing efforts, adding historical context, and patiently accepting revisions on the never-ending job of writing captions.

Once again I applaud my daughter, Susan Hammel Joyce, and my grandchildren, Danny and Caleigh Joyce, for cheering me on while this challenging project occupied me for almost two years.

It has been a fascinating journey.

Bette

Sources

GENERAL BACKGROUND AND INTRODUCTION

Borchert, John R., et al. *Legacy of Minneapolis, Preservation Amid Change*. Bloomington, MN: Voyageur Press, 1983.

Crotti, Nancy. "Minneapolis Chain of Lakes." "Homes" supplement clipping, *Star Tribune*, May [n.d.] 2011. Hennepin History Museum.

Durand, Paul. *Where the Waters Gather and the Rivers Meet: An Atlas of the Eastern Sioux*. Prior Lake: The author, 1994.

Glancy, Bob. Cedar-Isles calendars, 1992, 1996, 1998, 1999. Hennepin History Museum.

Irving, Robert M., and Kenneth Carley. "Horse Racing on Ice Was Popular in the Twin Cities." *Minnesota History* 41 (1969): 372.

Kaplan, Steven "The Lakes of Our Cities." *Star Tribune* Sunday Magazine, July 19, 1987.

Kennedy, Ernest J., Papers, 1910–30. Northwest Architectural Archives, University of Minnesota.

Lanegran, David A., and Ernest R. Sandeen. "The Calhoun-Isles Community." *The Lake District of Minneapolis*. 1979; reprint, Minneapolis: University of Minnesota Press, 2004.

Lathrop, Allan. *Minnesota Architects: A Biographical Dictionary*. Minneapolis: University of Minnesota Press, 2010.

McAlester, Virginia, and Lee McAlester. *A Field Guide to American Houses*. New York: Alfred A. Knopf, 2005.

Millett, Larry. *AIA Guide to the Minneapolis Lake District*. St. Paul: Minnesota Historical Society Press, 2009.

Minneapolis City Directory, 1859–2003. Minneapolis Collection, Hennepin County Library.

Minneapolis Collection. Hennepin County Library.

Minneapolis Park & Recreation Board. Details on individual parks and lakes available: www.minneapolisparks.org.

Pond, S. W. *Two Volunteer Missionaries Among the Dakota*. Boston: Congregational Sunday-School and Publishing Society, 1893.

Pond, Samuel L. *Dakota Life in the Upper Midwest*. 1908; reprint, St. Paul: Minnesota Historical Society Press, 1986.

Smith, David C. *City of Parks: The Story of Minneapolis Parks*. Minneapolis: Foundation for Minneapolis Parks, 2008.

Smith, David C. "Parks, Lakes, Trails and So Much More: An Overview of the Histories of MPRB Properties." Minneapolis Park & Recreation Board, 2008. Available: www.minneapolisparks.org/documents/parks/Parks_Lakes_Trails_Much_More.pdf.

Upham, Warren. *Minnesota Place Names: A Geographical Encyclopedia*. 1920; reprint, St. Paul: Minnesota Historical Society Press, 2001.

LAKE OF THE ISLES

THE SCRIVER | MCGANN-BURKE HOUSE

Glancy, Bob (known as the "Sherlock of Homes"). "A History of the Place Called 2631 East Lake of the Isles Parkway." Minneapolis: Privately published, September 2002. Copy in Hennepin History Museum.

Keith, Walter J. "Some Plaster Houses in the Northwest." *Keith's Magazine* (April 1910).

Koehler, Vance A. "A History of the Moravian Pottery and Tile Works." In *Moravian Tiles*, a sales catalog for the Moravian Pottery and Tile Works. 1913; reprint, Doylestown, PA: Bucks County Department of Parks and Recreation, 1999. Copy in homeowner's possession.

"Minneapolis, City of Parks and Homes." *The Western Architect* (December 1909).

Quigley, Tim, restoration architect. Interview.

THE CLIFFORD HOUSE

Goff, Lee. *Tudor Style: Tudor Revival Houses in America from 1890 to the Present*. New York: Universe, 2002.

Isern, Tom. "Plains Folk: Cream of Wheat." January 31, 2003. Available: www.ext.nodak.edu/extnews/newsrelease/2003/013003/04plains.htm.

Lathrop, Allan. *Minnesota Architects*.

McNeal, Jim, renovation architect. Interview.

Millett, Larry. *AIA Guide to the Minneapolis Lake District*.

THE FITERMAN | SKOGMO-MORIN HOUSE

Berry, Scott. "Introducing Architect Edwin Lundie" and "North Shore Retreats," exhibit panels, 2007. Lundie Room, Cross River Heritage Center, Schroeder, MN.

Lathrop, Allan. *Minnesota Architects*.

Millett, Larry. *AIA Guide to the Minneapolis Lake District*.

Mulfinger, Dale. *The Architecture of Edwin Lundie*. St. Paul: Minnesota Historical Society Press, 1995.

THE BULL | HIGGINS HOUSE

Bull, Webster. "Memories of Dad on Veteran's Day." November 11, 2011. Available: memoir sunlimited.blogspot.com/2011/11/memories-of-dad-on-veterans-day.html#more.

Calloway, Stephen, et al. *The Elements of Style: An Encyclopedia of Domestic Architectural Detail*. 1991; third ed., rev. and updated by Alan Powers. Buffalo, NY: Firefly Books, 2005.

Kennedy, Ernest J., Papers.

Martin, Lawrence A. "Thursday Night Hikes: Lake of the Isles Hike Architecture Notes, Part 1." Available: www.angelfire.com/mn/thursdaynighthikes/lakeisles_arch1.html.

Minneapolis City Directory, 1930. Reverse directory information for 2217 East Lake of the Isles Parkway.

Minneapolis Heritage Preservation Commission. "Lake of the Isles Historic District." Spring 1984. Minneapolis Collection, Hennepin County Library.

THE KERR | BACKUS | BARBER HOUSE

Backus, E. W., Portrait. Minneapolis Photo Collection, Hennepin County Library.

Calloway, Stephen, et al. *The Elements of Style*.

Lathrop, Allan. *Minnesota Architects*.

Millett, Larry. *AIA Guide to the Minneapolis Lake District*.

Minneapolis Heritage Preservation Commission. "Lake of the Isles Historic District."

THE SCHUTT | PRIEST HOUSE

Chrisman, Katherine. *Dreaming in the Dust: Restoring an Old House*. Boston: Houghton Mifflin, 1986.

"Elizabeth Ann Schutt (1903–1999) and The Friends of the Wild Flower Garden, Inc." Available: www.friendsofeloisebutler.org/pages/history/schutt.

"House History of 2100 James Avenue South." Minneapolis Collection, Hennepin County Library.

Keith, Walter J. *Historic Architecture for the Home Builder*. Minneapolis: The Keith Co., 1905.

Keith's Magazine on Home Building. Northwest Architectural Archives, University of Minnesota.

Kennedy and Van Dyck House Plans. Northwest Architectural Archives, University of Minnesota.

Lathrop, Allan. *Minnesota Architects*.

McAlester, Virginia, and Lee McAlester. *A Field Guide to American Houses*.

Photo of original house after 1926 addition and 1931 garage. In the possession of the Schutt family.

Photo of Schutt house, after 1931. Minneapolis Photo Collection, Hennepin County Library.

Saphir, Michael, landscape architect. Interview.

Ulland, Laurel, restoration architect. Interview.

THE KENNETH AND JUDY DAYTON HOUSE

Giovannini, Joseph. "Lakeside Villa by Vince James." *Architect: The Magazine of the American Institute of Architects* (July 1998).

James, Vincent, architect. Interview, 2011.

James, Vincent, and Jennifer Yoos. *VJAA: Vincent James Associates Architects*. New York: Princeton Architectural Press, 2006.

Lee, Jeffrey. "Obsessive, in a Good Way." *Architect: The Magazine of the American Institute of Architects* (May 17, 2011).

Ngo, Dung. "Dayton House." In *World House Now: Contemporary Architectural Directions*. New York: Universe, 2003.

THE MAPES HOUSE

Hyatt, Elizabeth, restoration architect. Interview.

Isern, Tom. "Plains Folk: Cream of Wheat."

Mapes, Emery. Biography. Minneapolis Collection, Hennepin County Library.

"Renovators." *Mpls./St. Paul* (April 1990).

Sundstrom, Ingrid. "Lake of the Isles Gem Rescued by Restorer." *Star Tribune*, May 28, 1988.

Seyb, Diana. "The Art of Restoring Older Homes." *Active Senior Lifestyles* (March 1987).

Vandam, Elizabeth A. *Harry Wild Jones: American Architect*. Minneapolis, Nodin Press: 2008.

THE DANAHER|WEESNER|MITCHELL HOUSE

"Car Collector Donald Weesner." *Star Tribune* clipping, May 1965. Minneapolis Collection, Hennepin County Library.

Danaher, Thomas F. *Minneapolis Journal* Index entries, 1913. Minneapolis Collection, Hennepin County Library.

Goff, Lee. *Tudor Style*.

Millett, Larry. *AIA Guide to the Minneapolis Lake District*.

Minneapolis Heritage Preservation Commission. "Lake of the Isles Historic District."

THE OWRE|WILLKIE HOUSE

Gebhard, David, and Tom Martinson. *Guide to the Architecture of Minnesota*. Minneapolis: University of Minnesota Press, 1978.

Heide, David, interior designer. Interview.

Legler, Dixie, and Christian Korab. *At Home on the Prairie: The Houses of Purcell & Elmslie*. San Francisco: Chronicle Books, 2006.

"Purcell Cutts House." *The Minnesotan* (March 1917). Hennepin History Museum.

Storrer, William Allin. *The Frank Lloyd Wright Companion*. Chicago: University of Chicago Press, 1993.

Torbert, Donald. "Significant Architecture in the History of Minneapolis." 1969. College of Design Library, University of Minnesota.

"Why Minneapolis Is Called the City of Beautiful Homes." Rotogravure series, *Minneapolis Journal*, April [n.d.] 1927.

THE FORD HOUSE

"Historical Society Given Documents," *Minneapolis Tribune* clipping, November [n.d.], 1965. Minneapolis Collection, Hennepin County Library.

Jedermann, Ruth M. "Allyn Kellogg Ford, Warmly Remembered." *Hennepin County History* (Fall 1964).

Klein, Marilyn W., and David P. Fogle. *Clues to American Architecture*. Washington, DC: Starrhill Press, 1986.

McAlester, Virginia, and Lee McAlester. *A Field Guide to American Houses*.

Minneapolis Heritage Preservation Commission. "Lake of the Isles Historic District."

"Prize Winners in Home Design Contest." *Minneapolis Journal* clipping, December [n.d.], 1929. Minneapolis Collection, Hennepin County Library.

Pesek Relative. Interview.

Safford, Virginia. "Cyril Pesek's Kitchen." *Minneapolis Star*, August 30, 1967.

Van Dyck, A. R. "Construction Documents for 2350 Lake of the Isles." June 23, 1928. In the possession of the homeowner.

THE MARTIN HOUSE

Calloway, Stephen, et al. *The Elements of Style*.

Elegant Homes, Timeless Style (spring/summer 2012).

Kirchner, William, former owner. Interview.

Minneapolis Heritage Preservation Commission. "Lake of the Isles Historic District."

McAlester, Virginia, and Lee McAlester. *A Field Guide to American Houses*.

Summerson, John M. *The Classical Language of Architecture*. London: Thames and Hudson, 1988.

THE AMSDEN|SANDBO HOUSE

Gebhard, David, and Tom Martinson. *Guide to the Architecture of Minnesota*.

Lanegran, David A., and Ernest R. Sandeen. "The Calhoun-Isles Community." *The Lake District of Minneapolis*.

Lathrop, Allan. *Minnesota Architects*.

McAlester, Virginia, and Lee McAlester. *A Field Guide to American Houses*.

Millett, Larry. *AIA Guide to the Minneapolis Lake District*.

Minneapolis Heritage Preservation Commission. "Lake of the Isles Historic District."

THE TWENTY-FIRST CENTURY HOUSE

Alt, Tim, architect. Interviews.

Architectural Record. Record Houses (2011).

Frampton, Kenneth. *Modern Architecture: A Critical History*. New York: Thames & Hudson, 1992.

Goldberger, Paul. "The Modernist Manifesto." *Preservation Magazine* (May/June 2008).

THE HALL | WEINER-WITTENBERG HOUSE

Eck, Jeremiah. *The Face of Home: A New Way to Look at the Outside of Your House.* Newton, CT: Taunton Press, 2006.

"James Stageberg Awarded the AIA Minnesota Gold Medal." *Architecture Minnesota* (November/December 1991).

Kudalis, Eric. "Profile of James Stageberg and His Designs as Part of a New Architecture in Postwar America." *Architecture Minnesota* (November/December 1992).

O'Connell, Kim. "Now Presenting ... the 20th Century." *Preservation Magazine* (May/June 2008).

Stageberg, James, and Susan Allen Toth. *A House of One's Own: An Architect's Guide to Designing the House of Your Dreams.* New York: Clarkson Potter, 1991.

Toth, Susan Allen (Mrs. James Stageberg), author. Interview.

THE SMITH | LIEPKE HOUSE

"Art and Craftwork." *Trends Magazine*, USA Kitchen Trends, 16.1A (1992).

Blake, Peter. *The Master Builders: Le Corbusier, Mies van der Rohe, and Frank Lloyd Wright.* New York: Norton & Company, 1996.

Lathrop, Allan. *Minnesota Architects.*

Legler, Dixie, and Christian Korab. *At Home on the Prairie.*

Metzler, Joseph G., restoration architect. Interview.

Storrer, William Allin. *The Frank Lloyd Wright Companion.*

Minneapolis Blue Book, 1917. Minneapolis Collection, Hennepin County Library.

Minneapolis City Directory, 1917. Minneapolis Collection, Hennepin County Library.

THE PURDY | WINSTON HOUSE

Mack, Linda. "If Only These Walls Could Talk." *Star Tribune*, November 23, 2000.

Porth, Andrew, architect. Interview.

Porth Architects, Ltd. Isle Addition Restoration Portfolio, 2000.

Purdy, Judge Milton, *Star Tribune* clippings, 1911. Minneapolis Collection, Hennepin County Library.

Vandam, Elizabeth A. *Harry Wild Jones.*

Winston, Frederick. Interview.

CEDAR LAKE

THE PETERSON HOUSE

Byer, Bill. "Time Tested: Highlights of Winston and Elizabeth Close's Modern Architecture." *Architecture Minnesota* (May/June 2012).

"Elizabeth Close, the New Gold Medalist." *Architecture Minnesota* (November/December, 2002).

Gebhard, David, and Tom Martinson. *Guide to the Architecture of Minnesota.*

Lathrop, Allan. *Minnesota Architects.*

THE KAUFMAN | LACEY HOUSE

Frampton, Kenneth. *Modern Architecture.*

Habich, John. "How a Globe-Trotting English Couple Found World Class Contentment on Cedar Lake." *Star Tribune*, August 27, 2003.

Heritage Preservation Commission, Minneapolis. Nomination Form for National Register of Historic Places: Kaufman House: Description and Significance. May 1982. Minneapolis City Planning Department.

Hitchcock, Henry Russell, and Philip Johnson. *The International Style.* 1932; reprint, New York: W. W. Norton, 1997.

"House for V. M. S. Kaufman, Minneapolis, Minn." *Architectural Forum* (April 1937).

Nuttgens, Patrick. *Understanding Modern Architecture.* London: Unwin Hyman, 1988.

Peterssen, Lars, architect. Interview.

Weeks, Kay D. "New Exterior Additions to Historic Buildings." In Department of the Interior, *The Preservation of Historic Architecture: The U.S. Government's Official Guidelines for Preserving Historic Homes.* Guilford, CT: Lyons Press, 2004.

THE NUMERO HOUSE

Bahe, Andrea. "James Dresser and the Art of Architecture." *At the Lake: Geneva Lakes Area Magazine* (Spring 2010).

Obituary for James Dresser. *Wisconsin Dells News*, January 28, 2011.

Obituary for Joseph Numero. *Star Tribune*, May 9, 1991.

Storrer, William Allin. *The Frank Lloyd Wright Companion.*

Thermo King Corporation Company History. Available: www.fundinguniverse.com/company-histories/Thermo-King-Corporation-company-History.html.

THE SCHIFMAN HOUSE

Fisher, Thomas. *The Invisible Element of Place: The Architecture of David Salmela.* Minneapolis: University of Minnesota Press, 2011.

Fisher, Thomas. "Rarified Air." *Architecture Minnesota* (November/December 2008).

Fisher, Thomas. *Salmela|Architect.* Minneapolis: University of Minnesota Press, 2005.

Gerloff, Robert, "Into the Woods." *Architecture Minnesota* (May/June 1998).

Martin, Frank Edgerton, ed. *Valued Places: Landscape Architecture in Minnesota.* Minneapolis: Minnesota Chapter, American Society of Landscape Architects, 2001.

Salmela, David, architect. Interview.

Schifman, Melissa, sustainability consultant. Interview.

Underwood, Lynn. "House Built from a Passion for Green." *Star Tribune*, May 8, 2011.

LAKE CALHOUN

THE HILLSIDE HOUSE

Girvin, Linda, interior designer. Interview.

Lathrop, Allan. *Minnesota Architects.*

LeFevre, Camille. *Charles R. Stinson Architects: Compositions in Nature.* Mulgrave, Victoria, Australia: Images Publishing, 2008.

LeFevre, Camille. "Loft at the Lake." *Midwest Home* (June/July 2010).

Stinson, Charles, architect. Interview.

COTTAGE CITY

Lanegran, David A., and Ernest R. Sandeen. "The Calhoun-Isles Community." *The Lake District of Minneapolis.*

Sullivan, Rhea, ed. *Down at the Lake: A History of Linden Hills and the Lake Harriet District.* Minneapolis: Linden Hills Study Group, 2001.

Sussman, Peter. "Cottage City 2011: Legacy & Future." Copy in author's possession.

LAKE HARRIET

THE LEJEUNE | MORGAN HOUSE

Eck, Jeremiah. *The Face of Home: A New Way to Look at the Outside of Your House.*

LeFevre, Camille. "2008 Architect of Distinction, Dan Nepp: Grown Up Whimsy." *Midwest Home* (March 2008).

Le Fevre, Camille. "2010 Architect of Distinction, Tom Ellison: Delighting with Impeccable Design." *Midwest Home* (April/May 2010).

"Midwest Marvel." *Homes On the Water*, A Meredith Special Interest Publication (spring/summer 2011).

THE WALLING | RUSSELL HOUSE

Lathrop, Allan. *Minnesota Architects*.

Millett, Larry. *AIA Guide to the Minneapolis Lake District*.

Minneapolis Heritage Preservation Commission. Landmarks, City of Minneapolis. National Register Designation, 1983; Local designation, 1987.

THE MADSEN | FITERMAN HOUSE

Klein, Marilyn W., and David P. Fogle. *Clues to American Architecture*.

Lathrop, Allan. *Minnesota Architects*.

McAlester, Virginia, and Lee McAlester. *A Field Guide to American Houses*.

Millett, Larry. *AIA Guide to the Minneapolis Lake District*.

Nuttgens, Patrick. *Simon and Schuster's Pocket Guide to Architecture*. London: Mitchell Beazley Publishing, 1980.

THE RAND | MCGLYNN-PHELPS HOUSE

"Architect Ernest Kennedy, Noted for His High Design." *The Improvement Bulletin*, January 14, 1938. Northwest Architectural Archives, University of Minnesota.

Calloway, Stephen, et al. *The Elements of Style*.

Haga, Chuck. "Seeking Shelter: A Survivalist Sect Leaves Lake Harriet for Montana." *Star Tribune*, April 17, 1990.

Lathrop, Allan. *Minnesota Architects*.

McAlester, Virginia, and Lee McAlester. *A Field Guide to American Houses*.

Millett, Larry. *AIA Guide to the Minneapolis Lake District*.

Nuttgens, Patrick. *Understanding Modern Architecture*.

Poppeliers, John C., et al. *What Style Is It?: A Guide to American Architecture*. Washington, DC: Preservation Press, 1983.

"The Rand House." *Twin Cities Reader* clipping, 1990. Minneapolis Collection, Hennepin County Library.

Index

Numbers in *italic* refer to pages
on which a photograph appears.

FRONTISPIECE: *Bull|Higgins House.*

PAGE IV, CLOCKWISE FROM UPPER LEFT:
Kerr|Backus|Barber House, Clifford House, Smith|Liepke House, Schifman House, Twenty-First Century House, Martin House.

PAGE V, CLOCKWISE FROM UPPER LEFT:
Purdy|Winston House, Twenty-First Century House, Madsen|Fiterman House, Clifford House, Bull|Higgins House, Hall|Weiner-Wittenberg House.

PAGE VIII: *Schutt|Priest House.*

PAGE 2: *Map by Map Hero.*

PAGE 213, CLOCKWISE FROM UPPER LEFT:
The Bull|Higgins House, The Owre|Willkie House, The Mapes House, The Scriver|McGann-Burke House, Elf House by Lake Calhoun, The Walling|Russell House.